A HISTORY AND GU

CRICKET WORLD CUP

To my mother and late father

A HISTORY AND GUIDE TO THE
CRICKET WORLD CUP

ANDREW ROBERTS

WHITE OWL

AN IMPRINT OF PEN & SWORD BOOKS LTD.
YORKSHIRE – PHILADELPHIA

First published in Great Britain in 2019 by
Pen & Sword White Owl
An imprint of
Pen & Sword Books Ltd
Yorkshire - Philadelphia

ISBN 978 1 52675 361 8

A CIP catalogue record for this book is available from the British Library.

Printed and bound in England by TJ International Ltd.
Typeset in Palatino 11/14 by
Aura Technology and Software Services, India

Pen & Sword Books Ltd incorporates the Imprints of Pen & Sword Books
Archaeology, Atlas, Aviation, Battleground, Discovery, Family History, History,
Maritime, Military, Naval, Politics, Railways, Select, Transport, True Crime,
Fiction, Frontline Books, Leo Cooper, Praetorian Press, Seaforth Publishing,
Wharncliffe and White Owl.

For a complete list of Pen & Sword titles please contact

PEN & SWORD BOOKS LIMITED
47 Church Street, Barnsley, South Yorkshire, S70 2AS, England
E-mail: enquiries@pen-and-sword.co.uk
Website: www.pen-and-sword.co.uk

or

PEN AND SWORD BOOKS
1950 Lawrence Rd, Havertown, PA 19083, USA
E-mail: uspen-and-sword@casematepublishers.com
Website: www.penandswordbooks.com

CONTENTS

ACKNOWLEDGEMENTS

I am very grateful to many people who have my first writing venture possible and would like to thank the following:

Vic Marks for so kindly writing the foreword. Vic probably did not realise that I would still be popping up forty years after he first taught me and he has had to suffer me at cricket dinners, in the Media Centre at Lord's when I made my BBC scoring debut and at grounds around England. It was a shame to me that England did not reach the 1983 final as it is very likely that Vic would have been the only cricketer to participate in a World Cup final on his birthday.

The late Bill Frindall, who transformed my life after meeting him at a cricket dinner in Westbury and later buying some of his score sheets of 'Massie's Match' at Lord's in 1972. The scoring method left me cold but awoke me four years later after being invited to become Bill's scorer based on my living close by and apparently being familiar with his system. It took me on various Maltamaniacs tours and led to scoring opportunities with the BBC and becoming a member of MCC.

Blundell's School, where I suspect I quickly became the cricket tragic. There were many opportunities there and the cricket I played there was amongst my happiest. My hero-worshipping of Geoffrey Boycott was tolerated with amusement and intrigue.

Ric Finlay at Tastats, for allowing me to use the excellent cricket statistics database. Ric has put up with my regular questions and technical deficiencies with good humour and I can wholeheartedly recommend Tastats (www.tastats.com.au) for its wide-ranging array of statistics and information.

John Hollands, who has been a great help with advice and guidance.

Rajesh Kumar, a well-known cricket statistician in Delhi, for years of friendship and hospitality and introducing me to many Indian players including my making a televised speech for M.S. Dhoni. Rajesh has taught me a lot about the print media in India and given me many fantastic opportunities including setting a quiz for the 2011 World Cup which was broadcast live on the giant screens at every match.

My mother and late father for their unfailing support and nurturing not only my interest in cricket but in all areas. I should also like to thank my mother for help with the proofreading and robust discussions about the use of hyphens.

Mark Kingstone, for offering sound advice when I asked for it whilst this book was in its early stage. He too collects books and keeps his in better condition.

Javed Qureshi for his help and suggestions. Cricket is a big part of his life, like mine.

Jonathan Wright, Heather Williams, Lori Jones, Carol Trow, Alice Wright, Emily Robinson and all at White Owl Publishing/Pen and Sword for not only giving me this opportunity but for making it fun and more straightforward than I had expected.

Despite vigorous checking, any errors are mine alone and should the book be reprinted, I shall ensure that any mistakes are corrected.

FOREWORD

by Vic Marks (England & Somerset)

One-day internationals can be forgettable affairs. In fact, the majority come into this category. But this does not apply when the World Cup comes around every four years.

We can argue about the format of the tournament and we often do. Is it too long? Are there enough/too many teams? But the beauty of the competition is that it matters. We remember the outcome of World Cups. The games have a special intensity, especially when we reach the knock-out stages.

So without blinking most of us – of a certain age – can recall the early domination of the West Indies, which was broken spectacularly and against all odds by India at Lord's in 1983; England's near misses at the hands of Australia and Pakistan in 1987 and 1992; the daring brilliance of Sri Lanka in 1996, which was followed by a long period of domination by Australia; the unfettered celebrations in Mumbai when India became the first side to win on home turf.

The broad landscapes of these tournaments linger in the memory. But some of the details remain hazy, which is where Andrew's book will be a wonderful aid. There is plenty of detail here as well as agonizing brain-teasers for the cricket nut. Andrew is an old pupil of mine, who has occasionally helped out on Test Match Special and he seems to have thrown himself into this project with even more enthusiasm than I remember in the classroom. The result is a fine piece of work which will keep you all entertained during the odd rain delay.

Vic Marks

INTRODUCTION

As almost continuous rain ended the Australian year of 1970 and began the New Year of 1971, the Third Test between Australia and England at Melbourne was abandoned on the third day after deliberation between the Australian Board and MCC

It was agreed that an extra Test would be added to England's already exhaustive itinerary and that the last day of this Third Test would be set aside for a one-day match of forty (eight-ball) overs. Thus was the first accepted One-Day International played on 5 January 1971 and the weather on that day had improved sufficiently to allow the match to be completed.

Not that the match was grandly reported upon in Wisden. At that stage in early 1971, no-one would have been aware of the jamboree which one-day international cricket would become and the 1972 Wisden gives a resume of the scores only in a match described as being between Australians and MCC.

As for the match, England were bowled out four balls short of their allotted forty overs for 190 with John Edrich top-scoring with 82. Ian Chappell, who had the distinction of hitting the first ODI six, made 60 and with Doug Walters contributing 41, the Australians won by five wickets with forty-two balls remaining. One-day cricket, in the form of the Midlands Knock-Out Competition (The Gillette Cup from 1963) had been played in England from 1962 and John Player's County League started in 1969 but this day in Melbourne in 1971 saw the more experienced one-day players defeated in front of almost 46,000 spectators.

In August 1972, the sides met again but this time in England after the exciting Test series had ended 2-all. Three one-day games of 55 overs per side were played for the Prudential Trophy, sponsored by the

Prudential Assurance Company, and with England winning the first match at Old Trafford by six wickets and Australia exacting revenge at Lord's by five wickets, the deciding game was played at Edgbaston.

Chasing just 180 to win the trophy, England had a fine start through Geoffrey Boycott and Dennis Amiss who added 76 for the first wicket. Wickets regularly fell and it required the ninth-wicket pair of Tony Greig and John Snow to take the hosts across the line and win the trophy and collect prize money of £2600, which included two Man of the Match awards and the Man of the Series award. Dennis Amiss, the Man of the Series recipient, scored the first ODI century in the first match at Old Trafford.

Just under six months later, Pakistan played New Zealand during the second half of their Antipodean tour having toured Australia first but without playing an ODI. This match, with 40 overs per side, was played at Christchurch between the Second and Third Tests.

Further 55-over matches were played during the English summer against their opponents, New Zealand and West Indies and 1974 saw India and Pakistan play two matches each on their tour of England, all playing for the Prudential Trophy. With New Zealand also embracing the format but over 35 overs, further matches were played against Australia and England so, by March 1975, a total of eighteen one-day international matches had been played since the hastily-convened Melbourne game of 5 January 1971.

At that stage, six batsmen had centuries to their names and Dennis Amiss already had two. David Lloyd's unbeaten 116 for England against Pakistan was the highest, whilst Pakistan's Majid Khan, Roy Fredericks of West Indies and New Zealanders Bevan Congdon and wicket-keeper Ken Wadsworth (who would die at the age of just 29 in 1976) had added to the centurions list.

Six bowlers had managed four wickets in an innings but the elusive fifth wicket had so far eluded everyone.

A significant event had taken place in England during June and July 1973, when cricketers from England, Australia, New Zealand, Trinidad and Tobago and Jamaica as well as an International XI and Young England side had contested matches which culminated in a World Cup final at Edgbaston on 28 July between England and Australia.

Enid Bakewell's 118 saw that England comfortably beat their opponents by 92 runs in the Women's World Cup competition.

On 26 July, the International Cricket Conference had approved a Test and County Cricket Board plan for all currently-playing Test countries to play a competition in England in 1975. The matches would be 60 overs per side and England was considered the desirable country to host it due to the light evenings and the potential of good weather. Matches could, though, be finished on a second or even third day should the good weather not appear and Prudential again provided the sponsorship.

The New Zealand and England match at Wellington on 9 March 1975 – which incidentally was rained off and abandoned after ten overs of England's pursuit of 228 resulting in the third No Result (all between the same two sides) – was the last match before the Prudential Cup started in England three months later.

COMPLETE WORLD CUP RESULTS FOR EACH COUNTRY 1975-2015

Country	Played	Won	Lost	Tied	NR	Win %	Finals	Trophies
AFGHANISTAN	6	1	5	0	0	16.67	0	0
AUSTRALIA	84	62	20	1	1	73.81	7	5
BANGLADESH	32	11	20	0	1	34.38	0	0
ENGLAND	72	41	29	1	1	56.94	3	0
INDIA	75	46	27	1	1	61.33	3	2
NEW ZEALAND	79	48	30	0	1	60.76	1	0
PAKISTAN	71	40	29	0	2	56.34	2	1
SOUTH AFRICA	55	35	18	2	0	63.64	0	0
SRI LANKA	73	35	35	1	2	47.95	3	1
WEST INDIES	71	41	29	0	1	57.75	3	2

MISCELLANY

- In eleven World Cup tournaments, a total of 169,831 (including 12,633 extras) runs have been scored for a loss of 5693 wickets making an average of 29.83 runs per wicket. There have been 165 centuries and 630 ducks scored. A total of 1057 players have represented their countries including four who have represented two.

- Twenty countries have participated in the history of the World Cup. In addition to those above contesting the 2019 competition, others are Bermuda, Canada, East Africa, Ireland, Kenya, Namibia, Netherlands, Scotland, United Arab Emirates and Zimbabwe.
- 103 grounds have been used including 20 in England.
- Australia, with 19,528 runs should become the first country to record 20,000 World Cup runs.

WORLD CUP RESULTS BY COUNTRY IN ENGLAND

Country	Played	Won	Lost	Tied	NR	Finals	Trophies
AFGHANISTAN	0	0	0	0	0	0	0
AUSTRALIA	24	13	10	1	0	2	1
BANGLADESH	3	1	2	0	0	0	0
ENGLAND	21	15	6	0	0	1	0
INDIA	22	11	11	0	0	1	1
NEW ZEALAND	22	10	11	0	1	0	0
PAKISTAN	24	12	12	0	0	1	0
SOUTH AFRICA	8	5	2	1	0	0	0
SRI LANKA	16	4	12	0	0	0	0
WEST INDIES	21	17	4	0	0	3	2

MISCELLANY

- Although West Indies will not play at The Oval, they have won all their five games there.
- Most World Cup team appearances at English grounds are Pakistan and Australia (5) at Headingley; West Indies (5) at The Oval; New Zealand (5) at Trent Bridge and India (5) at Old Trafford. England and Australia (5) share the honours at Lord's.

MATCH SCHEDULE AND HEAD-TO-HEAD IN THE WORLD CUP 1975-2015

1st MATCH | ENGLAND vs. SOUTH AFRICA
THE OVAL, 30 MAY

Played	Won by Eng	Won by SA	Ties	No Results
6	3	3	0	0

After readmission into international cricket just before the 1992 World Cup, South Africa reached the semi-finals against England only for a rain rule to end their chances of reaching the final. The two sides met at The Oval in 1999, South Africa winning easily after bowling England out for 103.

2nd MATCH | WEST INDIES vs. PAKISTAN
TRENT BRIDGE, 31 MAY

Played	Won by WI	Won by Pak	Ties	No Results
10	7	3	0	0

Despite their record above against West Indies, Pakistan came very close to toppling the eventual champions in both 1975 and 1979. A last-wicket unbeaten partnership of 64 between Deryck Murray and Andy Roberts saved West Indies in 1975. Pakistan did win the quarter-final match in 2011.

3rd MATCH | NEW ZEALAND vs. SRI LANKA
CARDIFF, 1 JUNE

Played	Won by NZ	Won by SL	Ties	No Results
10	4	6	0	0

Results have ebbed and flowed between the two sides through the World Cups. The sides have met twice in semi-finals (in 2007 and 2011), Sri Lanka winning both.

4th MATCH | AFGHANISTAN vs. AUSTRALIA
BRISTOL, 1 JUNE (D/N)

Played	Won by Afg	Won by Aus	Ties	No Results
1	0	1	0	0

In scoring the highest-ever total, 417 for six, Australia also secured the biggest runs victory (by 275 runs) against Afghanistan in 2015.

5th MATCH | SOUTH AFRICA vs. BANGLADESH
THE OVAL, 2 JUNE

Played	Won by SA	Won by Ban	Ties	No Results
3	2	1	0	0

Bangladesh sprung a surprise by beating South Africa at Providence in the 2007 competition with a 67-run victory.

6th MATCH | ENGLAND vs. PAKISTAN
TRENT BRIDGE, 3 JUNE

Played	Won by Eng	Won by Pak	Ties	No Results
9	4	4	0	1

Although the two teams have not met since the 2003 World Cup, there have been some fascinating matches. In 1979, England prevailed after scoring 165. They famously met twice in 1992 where rain saved Pakistan after being dismissed for just 74 at Adelaide. In the Melbourne final, however, Imran Khan's Pakistan side broke England's hearts by winning the trophy with a 22-run victory.

7th MATCH | AFGHANISTAN vs. SRI LANKA
CARDIFF, 4 JUNE

Played	Won by Afg	Won by SL	Ties	No Results
1	0	1	0	0

The teams have played each other three times in ODIs with Sri Lanka winning twice including a fairly tight World Cup match. Afghanistan did win the last meeting easily in the recent Asia Cup.

8th MATCH | SOUTH AFRICA vs. INDIA
SOUTHAMPTON, 5 JUNE

Played	Won by SA	Won by Ind	Ties	No Results
4	3	1	0	0

South Africa won the first three meetings between the teams, but India came back strongly at Melbourne in 2015 winning by 130 runs.

9th MATCH | BANGLADESH vs. NEW ZEALAND
THE OVAL, 5 JUNE (D/N)

Played	Won by Ban	Won by NZ	Ties	No Results
4	0	4	0	0

Despite losing all their games against New Zealand, the last match in Hamilton in 2015 was a tighter match with the Black Caps winning by just three wickets after chasing 289.

10th MATCH | AUSTRALIA vs. WEST INDIES
TRENT BRIDGE, 6 JUNE

Played	Won by Aus	Won by WI	Ties	No Results
9	4	5	0	0

It was initially West Indies all the way as they beat Australia on all four occasions including the inaugural final in 1975. Australia did first beat their opponents in a low-scoring game at Melbourne in 1992 and although West Indies came back to win at Jaipur in 1996, Australia have won the last three meetings in a very close 1996 semi-final at Mohali and in 1999 and 2007.

11th MATCH | PAKISTAN vs. SRI LANKA
BRISTOL, 7 JUNE

Played	Won by Pak	Won by SL	Ties	No Results
7	7	0	0	0

Whilst Pakistan has never beaten India in the World Cup, they have beaten Sri Lanka on all seven occasions. Three matches have been won by 15 runs or fewer although Pakistan have twice been victorious by over 100 runs. Only in 1992 has Pakistan chased a total. The sides have only met once since that game, in 2011 in Colombo.

12th MATCH | ENGLAND vs. BANGLADESH
CARDIFF, 8 JUNE

Played	Won by Eng	Won by Ban	Ties	No Results
3	1	2	0	0

Bangladesh's only loss to England was their first encounter in 2007 when England won by four wickets after requiring only 144. An unbeaten ninth-wicket partnership of 58 at Chittagong in 2011 saw the hosts win a see-saw match and in 2015, Bangladesh's 275 for seven proved enough to eliminate England.

13th MATCH | AFGHANISTAN vs. NEW ZEALAND
TAUNTON, 8 JUNE (D/N)

Played	Won by Afg	Won by NZ	Ties	No Results
1	0	1	0	0

The 2015 World Cup match at Napier saw the hosts comfortably score the 187 runs set by Afghanistan.

14th MATCH | INDIA vs. AUSTRALIA
THE OVAL, 9 JUNE

Played	Won by Ind	Won by Aus	Ties	No Results
11	3	8	0	0

Australia's better record includes their 2003 final victory against India after making 359 for two, the highest total in a final. India, however, won the 2011 quarter-final en route to a home victory. The two closest runs victories in the World Cup (1 run) have both been by Australia against India, at Madras in 1987 and Brisbane in 1992. Australia won the last meeting by 95 runs at Sydney in 2015. The sides also met at The Oval in 1999, Australia winning by 77 runs.

15th MATCH | SOUTH AFRICA vs. WEST INDIES
SOUTHAMPTON, 10 JUNE

Played	Won by SA	Won by WI	Ties	No Results
6	4	2	0	0

Although West Indies have only won two of their six games against South Africa, one was the 1996 quarter-final. The last match in 2015 at Sydney saw South Africa score 408 for five and win by 257 runs, the fourth-highest World Cup total and the joint-second largest runs victory.

16th MATCH | BANGLADESH vs. SRI LANKA
BRISTOL, 11 JUNE

Played	Won by Ban	Won by SL	Ties	No Results
3	0	3	0	0

Bangladesh have never come close to defeating Sri Lanka in the World Cup. Indeed, in their first meeting at Pietermaritzburg in 2003, Chaminda Vaas's first over hat-trick had Bangladesh reeling. Their last fixture, at Melbourne in 2015, saw Sri Lanka score 332 for one and win by 92 runs.

17th MATCH | AUSTRALIA vs. PAKISTAN
TAUNTON, 12 JUNE

Played	Won by Aus	Won by Pak	Ties	No Results
9	5	4	0	0

Fortunes have fluctuated for both teams, but Australia have won the knock-out matches. Although they lost earlier to Pakistan in the 1999 tournament, they won the final against the same opponents easily. They beat Pakistan in the 1987 semi-final en route to their first World Cup trophy as well as the 2015 quarter-final after which they notched up their fifth crown.

18th MATCH | INDIA vs. NEW ZEALAND
TRENT BRIDGE, 13 JUNE

Played	Won by Ind	Won by NZ	Ties	No Results
7	3	4	0	0

The sides have not met since India won in 2003 and until then, New Zealand predominantly held sway although India won twice in India during the 1987 World Cup.

19th MATCH | ENGLAND vs. WEST INDIES
SOUTHAMPTON, 14 JUNE

Played	Won by Eng	Won by WI	Ties	No Results
6	5	1	0	0

England enjoy a proud record against West Indies having not lost to them since 1979. The one defeat, though, was the 1979 final which, after subsequent appearances in the 1987 and 1992 finals, means that the coveted title still eludes them.

20th MATCH | SRI LANKA vs. AUSTRALIA
THE OVAL, 15 JUNE

Played	Won by SL	Won by Aus	Ties	No Results
9	1	7	0	1

The only sides to twice contest a final against each other, Sri Lanka's only win against Australia was in the 1996 final. The two sides also contested the 2007 final in Barbados, Australia winning comfortably by 53 runs. The most recent game, in 2015, saw Australia again win comfortably after scoring 376 for nine in Sydney in the match with the highest World Cup aggregate. The sides met in 1975 at The Oval before Sri Lanka gained Test status.

21st MATCH | SOUTH AFRICA vs. AFGHANISTAN
CARDIFF, 15 JUNE (D/N)

Played	Won by SA	Won by Afg	Ties	No Results
0	0	0	0	0

This will be the first occasion of both sides playing against each other in an ODI.

22nd MATCH | INDIA vs. PAKISTAN
OLD TRAFFORD, 16 JUNE

Played	Won by Ind	Won by Pak	Ties	No Results
6	6	0	0	0

Both teams only met in the World Cup for the first time in the 1992 campaign, but it has been India all the way. Both played against each other at Old Trafford in 1999, India comfortably defending 227. Their last meeting was at Adelaide in 2015, India scoring 300 for seven and winning by 76 runs.

23rd MATCH | WEST INDIES vs. BANGLADESH
TAUNTON, 17 JUNE

Played	Won by WI	Won by Ban	Ties	No Results
4	3	0	0	1

Bangladesh have not come close to defeating West Indies and in their last meeting at Dhaka in 2011, were bowled out for just 58 and lost by nine wickets.

24th MATCH | ENGLAND vs. AFGHANISTAN
OLD TRAFFORD, 18 JUNE

Played	Won by Eng	Won by Afg	Ties	No Results
1	1	0	0	0

England had few difficulties in their one meeting winning a rain-affected match at Sydney in 2015.

25th MATCH | NEW ZEALAND vs. SOUTH AFRICA
EDGBASTON, 19 JUNE

Played	Won by NZ	Won by SA	Ties	No Results
7	5	2	0	0

The two sides met previously at Edgbaston in 1999 which was one of the two occasions where New Zealand lost, on that occasion by 74 runs. New Zealand did win the last match in 2015 at Auckland which was the battle of the two sides to reach their first World Cup final.

26th MATCH | AUSTRALIA vs. BANGLADESH
TRENT BRIDGE, 20 JUNE

Played	Won by Aus	Won by Ban	Ties	No Results
2	2	0	0	0

Australia had few difficulties in winning both of their meetings against Bangladesh at Chester-le-Street in 1999 and Antigua in 2007.

27th MATCH | ENGLAND vs. SRI LANKA
HEADINGLEY, 21 JUNE

Played	Won by Eng	Won by SL	Ties	No Results
10	6	4	0	0

Despite a decent record against Sri Lanka, England have been beaten in the quarter-finals by Sri Lanka in the 1996 and 2011 tournaments. They also met at Headingley in 1983 where the hosts won by nine wickets.

28th MATCH | INDIA vs. AFGHANISTAN
SOUTHAMPTON, 22 JUNE

Played	Won by Ind	Won by Afg	Ties	No Results
0	0	0	0	0

This will be the first World Cup meeting these two sides. They have played each other twice in ODIs and Afghanistan forced a tie in the recent Asia Cup.

29th MATCH | WEST INDIES vs. NEW ZEALAND
OLD TRAFFORD, 22 JUNE (D/N)

Played	Won by WI	Won by NZ	Ties	No Results
7	3	4	0	0

The sides first met in the semi-final of the 1975 tournament, West Indies comfortably progressing to the final. There have been few tight games between the two but in 2015 New Zealand scored 393 for six in the quarter-final at Wellington. Martin Guptill's unbeaten 237 during that innings is the World Cup's highest individual score.

30th MATCH | PAKISTAN vs. SOUTH AFRICA
LORD'S, 23 JUNE

Played	Won by Pak	Won by SA	Ties	No Results
4	1	3	0	0

South Africa enjoyed the earlier exchanges, winning the first three matches including a low-scoring match in 1999. Pakistan have, however, won the last fixture at Auckland in 2015 by 29 runs.

31st MATCH | BANGLADESH vs. AFGHANISTAN
SOUTHAMPTON, 24 JUNE

Played	Won by Ban	Won by Afg	Ties	No Results
1	1	0	0	0

Bangladesh ran out comfortable winners in Afghanistan's first-ever World Cup match in 2015. In their seven ODIs against Bangladesh, Afghanistan have already beaten Bangladesh three times.

32nd MATCH | ENGLAND vs. AUSTRALIA
LORD'S, 25 JUNE

Played	Won by Eng	Won by Aus	Ties	No Results
7	2	5	0	0

England take on Australia at HQ having gained one of their two victories against their greatest opponents there in 1979 when they won by six wickets. The biggest match between the two opponents was the 1987 final at Eden Gardens, Calcutta where Australia prevailed by just seven runs.

33rd MATCH | NEW ZEALAND vs. PAKISTAN
EDGBASTON, 26 JUNE

Played	Won by NZ	Won by Pak	Ties	No Results
8	2	6	0	0

New Zealand may not enjoy the greatest record against Pakistan, but one of their two victories was at Edgbaston in 1983 when they won by 52 runs.

34th MATCH | WEST INDIES vs. INDIA
OLD TRAFFORD, 27 JUNE

Played	Won by WI	Won by Ind	Ties	No Results
8	3	5	0	0

West Indies' first loss was in the third World Cup to India at Old Trafford where they meet again in the 2019 tournament. Undoubtedly, India's most famous victory against the same opponents was later in 1983 when they won the final at Lord's by 43 runs against the odds.

35th MATCH | SRI LANKA vs. SOUTH AFRICA
CHESTER-LE-STREET, 28 JUNE

Played	Won by SL	Won by SA	Ties	No Results
5	1	3	1	0

It has predominantly been South Africa all the way in their head-to-head with Sri Lanka. They lost the first match at Wellington in 1992 but have won three of the last four games. The notable match was, though, the 2003 Durban tie which saw the hosts eliminated after a misreading of the Duckworth Lewis calculation.

36th MATCH | PAKISTAN vs. AFGHANISTAN
HEADINGLEY, 29 JUNE

Played	Won by Pak	Won by Afg	Ties	No Results
0	0	0	0	0

Although this will be the first World Cup meeting between the two teams, they have played against each other in three ODIs, Pakistan winning all of them.

37th MATCH | NEW ZEALAND vs. AUSTRALIA
LORD'S, 29 JUNE (D/N)

Played	Won by NZ	Won by Aus	Ties	No Results
10	3	7	0	0

Australia's better record includes the 2015 trophy spoiling New Zealand's first final appearance. An enthralling early stage match had seen the roles reversed, New Zealand scraping home by one wicket chasing just 152. The Antipodean countries first met in the 1987 World Cup, Australia winning by just three runs at Indore.

38th MATCH | ENGLAND vs. INDIA
EDGBASTON, 30 JUNE

Played	Won by Eng	Won by Ind	Ties	No Results
7	3	3	1	0

Both sides hold an even record against each other; three wins and the famous Bangalore tie in 2011. Other than the Bangalore match, none of the results have been especially close but it was at Edgbaston in 1999 where India defended 233 to eliminate England from their fourth home World Cup. Ashish Nehra's six for 23 at Durban in 2003 is still India's best bowling performance in the World Cup.

39th MATCH | SRI LANKA vs. WEST INDIES
CHESTER-LE-STREET, 1 JULY

Played	Won by SL	Won by WI	Ties	No Results
6	2	4	0	0

West Indies won the first four fixtures between the sides, but Sri Lanka have won the last two in 2003 and 2007.

40th MATCH | BANGLADESH vs. INDIA
EDGBASTON, 2 JULY

Played	Won by Ban	Won by Ind	Ties	No Results
3	1	2	0	0

Bangladesh's defeat of India in the 2007 competition led to India's early exit. India have won the last two fixtures in 2011 and 2015 comfortably.

41st MATCH | ENGLAND vs. NEW ZEALAND
CHESTER-LE-STREET, 3 JULY

Played	Won by Eng	Won by NZ	Ties	No Results
8	3	5	0	0

England won the first three meetings between the sides from 1975 but New Zealand have won the last five matches since 1983.

42nd MATCH | AFGHANISTAN vs. WEST INDIES
HEADINGLEY, 4 JULY

Played	Won by Afg	Won by WI	Ties	No Results
0	0	0	0	0

Although this will be the first meeting between the sides in the World Cup, Afghanistan has already defeated West Indies in three of their five ODIs, including two in World Cup qualifying which helped them make the competition proper.

43rd MATCH | PAKISTAN vs. BANGLADESH
LORD'S, 5 JULY

Played	Won by Pak	Won by Ban	Ties	No Results
1	0	1	0	0

The two teams have only met once but, famously, Bangladesh won by 62 runs at Northampton in 1999. A year later, they made their Test debut.

44th MATCH | SRI LANKA vs. INDIA
HEADINGLEY, 6 JULY

Played	Won by SL	Won by Ind	Ties	No Results
8	4	3	0	1

There have been many memorable meetings between the two teams. Sri Lanka first beat India in 1979 as an Associate nation before blitzing them in Delhi in 1996. They were later awarded the semi-final after crowd disturbance in Kolkata ended the match, sealing their place in the final. India responded with a big victory in Taunton in 1999 but the grandest meeting was the 2011 final in Mumbai where M.S. Dhoni's side successfully chased the Sri Lankan total of 274 for six.

45th MATCH | AUSTRALIA vs. SOUTH AFRICA
OLD TRAFFORD, 6 JULY (D/N)

Played	Won by Aus	Won by SA	Ties	No Results
5	3	1	1	0

South Africa's first match in the World Cup in 1992 saw them overwhelm holders, Australia, by nine wickets at Sydney. Both teams are remembered for the dramatic 1999 semi-final tie at Edgbaston after which Australia progressed to the final. The 1992 win remains South Africa's sole success against Australia.

46th MATCH | SEMI-FINAL* 1st vs. 4th
OLD TRAFFORD, 9 JULY

47th MATCH | SEMI-FINAL* 2nd vs. 3rd
EDGBASTON, 11 JULY

48th MATCH | FINAL*
LORD'S, 14 JULY

*Both semi-finals and final have a reserve day.

A HISTORY
OF THE
WORLD CUP

1975

There was much anticipation at the first official men's World Cup, officially called the Prudential Cup.

The six current playing Test nations of England, Australia, New Zealand, India, Pakistan and West Indies were joined by Sri Lanka and East Africa in a two-week tournament which started on 7 June and finished with the final at Lord's on 21 June. The eight teams were divided into two groups of four and each would play the other group sides with the top two qualifying for the semi-finals.

The tournament consisted of fifteen games with four played on 7, 11 and 14 June, the semi-finals on 18 June and the final on 21 June. 60 overs were allowed per side.

All the teams were invited to a reception at Buckingham Palace hosted by the Queen, HRH Prince Philip (who would also later hand over the trophy to the winning captain) and HRH Prince Charles.

The weather stayed fine for the entire two week period, meaning that all games were completed on the day they started so there was no recourse for play going into an extra day. The first day saw England take on India at Lord's, Australia played Pakistan at Headingley, Sri Lanka made their Limited-Overs International debut against West Indies at Old Trafford and New Zealand faced East Africa at Edgbaston. Before the World Cup, the highest total in the previous eighteen Limited-Overs International was England's 266 for six against India at Headingley the previous year yet, by 8 June 1975, three of the participating teams had bettered this.

A bizarre match at Lord's saw England rack up 334 for four with Dennis Amiss adding his third ODI century before being dismissed for 137. With Keith Fletcher contributing 68 in a second wicket partnership of 176 with Amiss, England reached an impressive total.

The 20,000 crowd were probably not surprised that England won comfortably but the margin of victory, 202 runs, was even more remarkable given that India only lost three wickets before their overs ran out with their total on just 132. Sunil Gavaskar's unbeaten and notorious 36 in 174 balls remains the lowest scoring rate by an Indian batsman in their World Cup history. The other unbeaten batsman, Brijesh Patel, with 16 not out in 57 balls, retains India's second-lowest scoring rate.

West Indies showed vast superiority over the non-Test playing nation, Sri Lanka. Invited to bat first, Sri Lanka could manage only 86 with their tenth wicket pair of Somachandra de Silva and Lalith Kaluperuma sharing in a partnership of 28, the highest of the innings. West Indies reached their target in just the twenty-first over by nine wickets.

Australia started strongly against Pakistan reaching 278 for seven with Ross Edwards top-scoring with an unbeaten 80. Fifties from Majid Khan and captain Asif Iqbal kept Pakistan in the hunt but Dennis Lillee's five for 34 not only gave Australia victory by 73 runs but made the bowler the first to take five wickets in an ODI innings.

At Birmingham, New Zealand's captain, Glenn Turner, added a century to follow Amiss's and finished with an unbeaten 171 – the highest ODI score at that stage – in his side's 309 for five. East Africa survived their sixty overs but, at 128 for eight, were 181 runs adrift of their target.

East Africa may not have made many runs in their only World Cup appearance, but they survived for over fifty overs in each of their three innings. There were some interesting bowling figures against them, with Bishan Bedi returning extraordinary figures of 12-8-6-1 for India. Richard Hadlee was little less impressive with 12-6-10-0 in New Zealand's victory whilst John Snow took four for 11 in 12 overs for England.

The four matches played on 11 June contained some fascinating play. At Edgbaston, Pakistan's 266 for seven seemed to be ample as West Indies lost their ninth wicket at 203. Deryck Murray, batting at eight, and fast bowler Andy Roberts managed, amidst much tension, to add the necessary 64 runs in 13 overs to win the match for West Indies with just two balls remaining. Their partnership remains the highest for the tenth wicket in a winning side.

England also scored 266 but for six wickets at Trent Bridge against New Zealand, though they enjoyed a smoother ride, dismissing their opponents for 186 to win by 80 runs. Keith Fletcher was Man of the Match for his 131.

The highest aggregate was achieved between Australia and Sri Lanka in a match which saw 604 runs scored for just nine wickets. A record partnership for any wicket at that stage of 182 between

Rick McCosker (73) and Alan Turner (101) saw the match favourites total 328 for five. Sri Lanka batted spiritedly and ended up with a highly creditable 276 for four by the time their overs were exhausted, but Jeff Thomson had forced Duleep Mendis and Sunil Wettimuny to retire hurt and both were taken to hospital.

East Africa succumbed easily to India at Headingley, losing by 10 wickets after managing just 120. Sunil Gavaskar atoned for his Lord's performance by outscoring his partner, Farokh Engineer, in making an unbeaten 65 in 86 balls as India won with over half of their overs remaining.

Of the remaining matches which led to the semi-finals, England had an easy victory over East Africa by 196 runs and Glenn Turner continued his fine form with another unbeaten hundred in New Zealand's defeat of India. Pakistan enjoyed a 192-run win over Sri Lanka, but the best game came at The Oval between the fancied West Indies and Australia. Although it was not close, Alvin Kallicharran's 78, which included an assault of 35 runs in 10 balls on Lillee, took West Indies to an easy, seven wicket victory with 14 overs remaining.

Group A winners, England, met the runners-up of Group B, Australia, at Headingley whilst Group B winners, West Indies, took on Group A runners-up, New Zealand, at The Oval in the semi-finals. The match at Headingley has lived long in the memory and must rank as one of the greatest World Cup matches. On winning the toss, Ian Chappell asked England to bat first on a green-looking pitch which suited Gary Gilmour ideally. Playing in just his third ODI and first World Cup match, Gilmour was preferred to Jeff Thomson to open the bowling and, bowling his twelve overs straight through, finished with 12-6-14-6 as England crumbled to 37 for seven.

Captain Mike Denness, with assistance from John Snow, Geoff Arnold and Peter Lever, helped shepherd the total to 93 before Lever was last out. With a bowling attack comprising the three latter-mentioned batsmen and Yorkshire all-rounder, Chris Old, there was still every chance that England might pull off a remarkable victory.

Although Australia started reasonably, they did reach 32 for two before a dramatic collapse saw them lose three further wickets on that score and Ross Edwards at 39, Old taking three quick wickets and Snow two. It was, though, Gilmour's day as, with Doug Walters, he helped add an unbeaten 55 – the highest and only fifty partnership of the match – as Australia reached the final without further loss. The match had lasted just 65 of the scheduled 120 overs.

The second semi-final was less fraught, with New Zealand being dismissed for 158 after reaching some degree of prosperity at 98 for one. Bernard Julien continued his fine World Cup to that point with his second four wicket haul. Although they lost five wickets in reaching their target, West Indies were never in much danger, especially after a second-wicket partnership of 125 between Gordon Greenidge and Kallicharran.

On a glorious London day, West Indies met Australia in the first ever World Cup final in front of 26,000 spectators. Ian Chappell again won the toss and asked West Indies to bat first and his decision seemed to have been vindicated when Roy Fredericks, Greenidge and Kallicharran were dismissed by the time the total had reached 50.

Captain Clive Lloyd, in partnership with the 39-year-old Rohan Kanhai, took on the might of the Australian bowlers, adding 149 in 36 overs and seizing the initiative. Lloyd reached a wonderful hundred in just 82 balls before being dismissed by Gilmour, who continued his fine form of Headingley in finishing with five for 48 after again opening the bowling. Late hitting from Keith Boyce, Julien and Murray gave the West Indies a very healthy 291 for eight.

Viv Richards made his ODI debut in the World Cup and whilst making few runs, made an impact in this final running out three batsmen at vital periods. Ian Chappell top-scored with 62 and indeed eight other batsmen made between 11 and 40 but the need to keep on top of a daunting total led to five batsmen being run out.

Even the last pair of Lillee and Thomson batted spiritedly after coming in requiring 59 runs. They continued running whilst the crowd spilled on to the field thinking mistakenly that the last wicket had been taken. It was shortly afterwards – inevitably to the fifth and final run out – and just before 9 pm the Prudential Trophy was handed to Clive Lloyd by HRH Prince Philip after his side's 17-run win.

1975 MISCELLANY

- Six of the World Cup's first 15 individual slowest scoring rates (based on facing 50 balls in an innings) were recorded in 1975, East Africa's Harilal Shah's six in 53 balls against England being the slowest.
- There have been only six instances in World Cup history of bowlers bowling ten or more overs in an innings at less than a run per over. Three occurred in 1975 and all were against East Africa: Bishan Bedi's

12-8-6-1 for India; Richard Hadlee's 12-6-10-0 for New Zealand and John Snow's 12-6-11-4 for England.

- Australia's Gary Gilmour is the only bowler to take five or more wickets in both a World Cup semi-final and final. Both came in successive matches and only Sri Lanka's Ashantha de Mel has taken five wickets in successive World Cup matches. Gilmour would play just one further ODI after the final.
- Australia are the only team to lose five wickets to run outs in a World Cup innings twice. After the 1975 final, the same happened to them in Mumbai against India in 1996.
- The unbeaten stand of 64 between Deryck Murray and Andy Roberts is the highest partnership made in a World Cup match by the tenth wicket pair. The same has only happened on one other occasion when Pakistan's Saqlain Mushtaq and Shoaib Akhtar added 54 against England at Cape Town in 2003.
- 1975 is the only occasion of both captains passing 50 in the same World Cup final.
- Sri Lanka's Somachandra de Silva celebrated his 33rd birthday during his team's match against Australia. He would repeat the experience against England in the 1983 World Cup. Bas Zuiderent of the Netherlands, Pakistan's Shahid Afridi and New Zealand's Ross Taylor have also celebrated two World Cup birthday matches.
- East Africa's Frasat Ali is one of only two players to open both the batting and bowling in every match of their World Cup career. Netherland's Darron Reekers, in 2007, is the other. Frasat is also East Africa's sole six-hitter.
- The seven East African batsmen dismissed bowled against England is a record for a World Cup match.
- West Indian batsman, Roy Fredericks, was the first player to be dismissed hit wicket in an ODI and is the only player to be so dismissed in a World Cup final.

1975 STATISTICS

HIGHEST TOTALS	
334 for 4 in 60 overs	England vs. India at Lord's
330 for 6 in 60 overs	Pakistan vs. Sri Lanka at Nottingham
328 for 5 in 60 overs	Australia vs. Sri Lanka at The Oval

HIGHEST TOTALS

309 for 5 in 60 overs	New Zealand vs. East Africa at Birmingham
291 for 8 in 60 overs	West Indies vs. Australia at Lord's

LOWEST COMPLETED TOTALS

86 in 37.2 overs	Sri Lanka vs. West Indies at Manchester
93 in 36.2 overs	England vs. Australia at Leeds
94 in 52.3 overs	East Africa vs. England at Birmingham

HIGHEST MATCH AGGREGATES

604 for 9 wickets	Australia (328-5) vs. Sri Lanka (276-4) at The Oval
565 for 18 wickets	West Indies (291-8) vs. Australia (274) at Lord's
533 for 16 wickets	Pakistan (266-7) vs. West Indies (267-9) at Birmingham

LOWEST MATCH AGGREGATES WITH RESULTS

173 for 11 wickets	Sri Lanka (86) vs. West Indies (87-1) at Manchester
187 for 16 wickets	England (93) vs. Australia (94-6) at Leeds
243 for 10 wickets	East Africa (120) vs. India (123-0) at Leeds

BIGGEST VICTORY MARGINS

202 runs	England (334-4) vs. India (132-3) at Lord's
196 runs	England (290-5) vs. East Africa (94) at Birmingham
192 runs	Pakistan (330-6) vs. Sri Lanka (138) at Nottingham
181 runs	New Zealand (309-5) vs. East Africa (128-8) at Birmingham
10 wickets	India (123-0) vs. East Africa (120) at Leeds
9 wickets	West Indies (87-1) vs. Sri Lanka (86) at Manchester

LOWEST VICTORY MARGINS

17 runs	West Indies (291-8) vs. Australia (274) at Lord's
1 wicket	West Indies (267-9) vs. Pakistan (266-7) at Birmingham

LEADING RUN SCORERS

333 (average 166.50)	Glenn Turner (New Zealand)
243 (average 60.75)	Dennis Amiss (England)

HIGHEST SCORERS		
171*	Glenn Turner	New Zealand vs. East Africa at Birmingham
137	Dennis Amiss	England vs. India at Lord's
131	Keith Fletcher	England vs. New Zealand at Nottingham
114*	Glenn Turner	New Zealand vs. India at Manchester
102	Clive Lloyd	West Indies vs. Australia at Lord's
101	Alan Turner	Australia vs. Sri Lanka at The Oval

CENTURIES
Six

LEADING WICKET TAKERS	
11 (average 5.64)	Gary Gilmour (Australia)
10 (average 17.70)	Bernard Julien (West Indies)
10 (average 18.50)	Keith Boyce (West Indies)

BEST BOWLING PERFORMANCES		
12-6-14-6	Gary Gilmour	Australia vs. England at Leeds
12-2-34-5	Dennis Lillee	Australia vs. Pakistan at Leeds
12-2-48-5	Gary Gilmour	Australia vs. West Indies at Lord's

FIVE WICKETS IN AN INNINGS
Three

HIGHEST PARTNERSHIPS FOR EACH WICKET				
1	182	Alan Turner & Rick McCosker	Aus. vs. SL	The Oval
2	176	Dennis Amiss & Keith Fletcher	Eng. vs. Ind	Lord's
3	149	Glenn Turner & John Parker	NZ vs. EAf	Birmingham
4	149	Rohan Kanhai & Clive Lloyd	WI vs. Aus	Lord's
5	89*	Mike Denness & Chris Old	Eng. vs. Ind.	Lord's
6	99	Ross Edwards & Rod Marsh	Aus. vs. WI	The Oval
7	55*	Doug Walters & Gary Gilmour	Aus. vs. Eng.	Leeds
7	55	Syed Abid Ali & Madan Lal	Ind. vs. NZ	Manchester
8	48	Brian McKechnie & Dayle Hadlee	NZ vs. Eng.	Nottingham
9	60	Syed Abid Ali & Srinivas Venkataraghavan	Ind. vs.NZ	Manchester
10	64*	Deryck Murray & Andy Roberts	WI vs. Pak	Birmingham

1979

The 1979 World Cup returned to England once again for much the same reasons as the 1975 edition. As the 1975 tournament had been such a success, it was hoped that the weather would again play ball and the format remained the same to the one used four years previously. It was still known as the Prudential Cup.

The same Test nations were again represented as were Sri Lanka and Canada, both of whom had reached the ICC final and thereby qualified from a three-group tournament. Fifteen matches of 60 overs per side would again be played and there would be four matches due to be played on 9, 13 and 16 June with both semi-finals on 20 June and the final on 23 June. The weather turned fickle for the middle set of group matches with only one of the four matches being completed on 13 June. Two games required two days play and another was abandoned after no play on all three.

Group A was contested between England, Australia, Pakistan and Canada whilst Group B saw West Indies, India, New Zealand and Sri Lanka pitted against each other.

The holders, West Indies, made an impressive start at Edgbaston against India with a nine-wicket victory and eight-and-a-half overs remaining. Seven Indian batsmen reached double figures but only Gundappa Viswanath held the West Indian pace attack at bay in making 75 in their total of 190. Extras was India's second highest scorer. An opening partnership of 138 between Greenidge, who finished unbeaten on 106, and Desmond Haynes, saw West Indies make not only a formidable start but set the benchmark for anyone wishing to challenge them.

Although it was a low-scoring game at Lord's, England and Australia was a closer game than the scores suggested. Despite reaching comparative prosperity at 97 for one after being put in to bat, Australia could ultimately only manage 159 for nine in their full quota of overs. Suffering from another bout of run outs, the surprising feature was that England's most successful bowler was Geoff Boycott with two for 15 in six overs. Bizarrely, he would take more wickets than he made runs in this match as England, after a poor start, rallied through Mike Brearley and Graham Gooch as they won by six wickets.

Canada's international bow against Pakistan started promisingly through Glenroy Sealy and a Canadian-born (and unrelated) Chappell with an opening stand of 54 but ultimately, their challenge fizzled out with an eight-wicket defeat after setting just 140.

With Glenn Turner again impressing after his 1975 performances, New Zealand comfortably beat Sri Lanka at Trent Bridge to end the first round of matches.

The bad weather affected the second round of matches with only New Zealand and India at Headingley being completed on 13 June. India's poor showing in both World Cups was further compounded with an eight-wicket defeat after setting only 183. Despite an opening partnership of 100, New Zealand only reached their target with three overs to spare through an unbeaten 84 from Bruce Edgar and 43 not out from Turner, batting other than as an opener for the first time in his ODI career.

Other weather in the north was not so kind, two matches requiring a second day to obtain a result. Australia's poor tournament continued at Trent Bridge to Pakistan with an 89-run defeat. Eight Pakistan batsmen reached double figures in their 286 for seven and despite 72 from opener Andrew Hilditch, Australia were bowled out for 197 on the second day.

A more dramatic match at Old Trafford produced just 91 runs but, after the first day was rained off, the game was fortunate not to reach a third day. Canada, dismissed for just 45, resisted for 40.3 overs but there were some interesting bowling figures, the best being Chris Old's four for eight in 10 overs and Bob Willis's four for 11 in 10.3.

Canada quickly took two wickets but eventually the sun reappeared and England reached their target without further ado. The match is the second-lowest aggregate in World Cup history and Canada's run rate the lowest in all World Cup tournaments.

The inclement weather was not restricted to the north as The Oval suffered three blank days before the West Indies and Sri Lanka game was abandoned with two points awarded to each side. This put the West Indian semi-final place in possible doubt should they have subsequently lost to New Zealand and if Sri Lanka could then upset India. The slot would then be determined by run rate.

In the last round of matches, Sri Lanka did indeed pull off the upset by defeating India at Old Trafford to become the first non-Test playing nation to beat a Test side. Three Sri Lankans passed fifty and two de Silvas shared five wickets as the Associate side comfortably defended 238.

West Indies did ultimately prevail against New Zealand at Trent Bridge rendering run rate superfluous. Not everything went entirely to plan but, after Lloyd's unbeaten 73 had taken West Indies to 244 for seven, their formidable quintet of fast bowlers restricted New Zealand to 212 for nine.

Australia had little difficulty against Canada at Edgbaston reaching their victory target of 106 with seven wickets and 34 overs in hand. The Canadians had started in a blaze of glory, Rodney Hogg being forced out of the attack after bowling two overs for 26 runs. Alan Hurst restored order with five for 21.

In dismissing Rick Darling, John Valentine could take home cherished memories of claiming an international opener in each of Canada's matches following his success in taking the wickets of Majid Khan and Mike Brearley in earlier matches.

One of the best matches of the tournament took place at Headingley, where England struggled with the bat after being put in. That they reached 165 was due in no small part to a ninth-wicket partnership of 43 between Willis and Bob Taylor. Majid Khan's three for 27 was his best ODI bowling performance.

In reply, Pakistan reached 27 before Mike Hendrick reduced them to an astonishing 34 for six with a spell of four wickets for three runs in eight balls. A captain's knock of 51 by Asif Iqbal and lower order contributions from Wasim Raja, Imran Khan and Wasim Bari took Pakistan tantalisingly close before Boycott, continuing his fine tournament form with the ball if not the bat, took the last two wickets to secure a 14-run victory. Both sides still progressed to the semi-finals where England played New Zealand and Pakistan contested the match at The Oval against West Indies.

At Old Trafford, fine bowling from New Zealand restricted England to a modest 221 for eight with Brearley making 53 and Gooch a more rapid 71. Derek Randall's unbeaten 42 at number seven proved invaluable in setting the opposition as many as England did.

In response, as many as eight New Zealand batsmen reached double figures but only opener, John Wright, passed fifty. Geoff Howarth became the fifth victim of Boycott's campaign and despite keeping in touch with England's score, 14 from the last over proved just beyond New Zealand as England crept into the final by just nine runs. It was a further blow to New Zealand who had shown once again that they could reach the semi-finals only to miss out on the final. It was a pattern which would continue.

West Indies returned to The Oval where they enjoyed play against Pakistan in a match which saw them through to their second consecutive final by the end of the day. Pakistan's decision to field was not met with immediate success, as Greenidge and Haynes plundered 132, their second century partnership of the tournament. With significant contributions from most in the order, West Indies finished with an imposing 293 for six. In what would be his final ODI, Asif Iqbal returned his best figures of four for 56.

Through a second-wicket partnership of 166 between Majid Khan and Zaheer Abbas, there were most certainly moments of concern for the defending champions when Pakistan had reached 176 for one. The battery of fast bowlers, especially Roberts and Colin Croft, made inroads and Richards's three wickets saw Pakistan's hopes dashed with ultimately a relatively comfortable 43-run win.

Whilst West Indies returned to Lord's, England appeared in a final for the first time and asked West Indies to bat first, albeit without an injured Willis. In the 1975 final, West Indies had struggled to 50 for three before finishing on 291 for eight. This time, their start was equally precarious and with Chris Old dismissing the hero of the first final, Clive Lloyd, through a remarkable caught and bowled, the defending champions were still short of the hundred.

On this occasion, it was Viv Richards who rose to the occasion and his second ODI hundred (and first in the World Cup) saw that the West Indies again, at 286 for nine, ended with an impressive total. After Lloyd's dismissal, it was Collis King who played one of the memorable World Cup innings also with 86 from just 66 balls in a partnership of 139 with Richards who finished on 138 not out. King hit three sixes and 10 fours and, for the first time in the competition, Boycott, still bowling around the wicket and wearing a cap, was treated disdainfully as were the other fill-in bowlers of Wayne Larkins and Gooch.

Brearley and Boycott (now more safely ensconced in a helmet) gave England a fine if laboured start and set a platform but, by the time they were parted at 129, 38 of the 60 overs had already been used. Both openers, who would only play in this one World Cup, bowed out with their highest World Cup scores but it left the stroke makers with a daunting task.

Although Gooch saw England to 183 for two, the ever-increasing run rate was making a successful defence of the West Indian trophy more than likely. So it was to prove as, in the quest of very quick runs, Joel Garner, wicketless after nine overs, returned to finish with five for 38 in 11 and clean bowling four of his victims as England folded for 194. Shortly afterwards, Clive Lloyd was holding up the Prudential Cup for the second time.

1979 MISCELLANY

- Canada became the first team on full ODI debut to open with a fifty partnership. Chris Chappell and Glenroy Sealy were the opening pair.
- The 91-run match aggregate between England and Canada is the second-lowest in World Cup history (with a result) behind the 73 between Canada (36) and Sri Lanka (37-1) at Paarl in 2003.
- Indian captain in both the 1975 and 1979 World Cups, Srinivas Venkataraghavan, went through both tournaments wicketless.
- The Boycott and Brearley 129-run partnership in the final was made from the fourth-lowest completed total to include a century partnership. The lowest in any World Cup game is 175 all out by United Arab Emirates against West Indies at Napier in 2015 and the lowest in a final was also in 2015 at Melbourne for New Zealand (183) against Australia.
- The five ducks in England's innings is the most in a World Cup final although the same number has been achieved in six other matches.
- Viv Richards's unbeaten 138 is the only occasion of the highest score in a World Cup tournament being in the final.
- Pakistan's Zaheer Abbas, for the second successive World Cup, was the only batsman to be dismissed in the 90s.

1979 STATISTICS

HIGHEST TOTALS	
293 for 6 in 60 overs	West Indies vs. Pakistan at The Oval
286 for 7 in 60 overs	Pakistan vs. Australia at Nottingham
286 for 9 in 60 overs	West Indies vs. England at Lord's

LOWEST COMPLETED TOTALS	
45 in 40.3 overs	Canada vs. England at Manchester
105 in 33.2 overs	Canada vs. Australia at Birmingham

HIGHEST MATCH AGGREGATES	
543 for 16 wickets	West Indies (293-6) vs. Pakistan (250) at The Oval
483 for 17 wickets	Pakistan (286-7) vs. Australia (197) at Nottingham
480 for 19 wickets	West Indies (286-9) vs. England (194) at Lord's

LOWEST MATCH AGGREGATES WITH RESULT	
91 for 12 wickets	Canada (45) vs. England (46-2) at Manchester
211 for 13 wickets	Canada (105) vs. Australia (106-3) at Birmingham

BIGGEST VICTORY MARGINS	
92 runs	West Indies (286-9) vs. England (194) at Lord's
89 runs	Pakistan (286-7) vs. Australia (197) at Nottingham
9 wickets	New Zealand (190-1) vs. Sri Lanka (189) at Nottingham
9 wickets	West Indies (194-1) vs. India (190) at Birmingham

LOWEST VICTORY MARGINS	
9 runs	England (221-8) vs. New Zealand (212-9) at Manchester
14 runs	England (165-9) vs. Pakistan (151) at Leeds
6 wickets	England (160-4) vs. Australia (159-9) at Lord's

LEADING RUN SCORERS

253 (average 84.33)	Gordon Greenidge (West Indies)
217 (average 108.50)	Viv Richards (West Indies)
210 (average 52.50)	Graham Gooch (England)

HIGHEST SCORES

138*	Viv Richards	West Indies vs England at Lord's
106*	Gordon Greenidge	West Indies vs. India at Birmingham

CENTURIES

Two

LEADING WICKET TAKERS

10 (average 14.90), Mike Hendrick (England)

BEST BOWLING PERFORMANCES

10-3-21-5	Alan Hurst	Australia vs. Canada at Birmingham
11-0-38-5	Joel Garner	West Indies vs. England at Lord's

FIVE WICKETS IN AN INNINGS

Two

HIGHEST PARTNERSHIPS FOR EACH WICKET

1	138	Gordon Greenidge & Desmond Haynes	WI vs. Ind.	Birmingham
2	166	Majid Khan & Zaheer Abbas	Pak. vs. WI	The Oval
3	108	Mike Brearley & Graham Gooch	Eng. vs. Aus.	Lord's
4	71	Andrew Hilditch & Graham Yallop	Aus. vs. Pak	Nottingham
5	139	Viv Richards & Collis King	WI vs. Eng	Lord's
6	40	Sunil Gavaskar & Kapil Dev	Ind. vs. NZ	Leeds
7	52	Asif Iqbal & Wasim Raja	Pak. vs. Eng	Leeds
8	41	Derek Randall & Bob Taylor	Eng. vs. NZ	Manchester
9	43	Bob Taylor & Bob Willis	Eng. vs. Pak	Leeds
10	27	Srinivas Venkataraghavan & Bishan Bedi	Ind. vs. WI	Birmingham

1983

The 1983 competition, sponsored by Prudential Assurance for the last time, adopted a slightly different format. A larger number of matches, twenty-seven, was played and each of the eight teams would play each other twice in the group stages. Each game would again consist of sixty overs per side, even though many ODI games in other countries were being played over fifty.

The groups saw England, Pakistan, New Zealand and Sri Lanka in Group A whilst West Indies, India, Australia and Zimbabwe contested Group B. Sri Lanka was by now a Test playing nation and Zimbabwe's inclusion was due to their winning the ICC Trophy in 1982.

A slightly longer period was set aside to allow for the increase in matches and generally the weather was again fine, with twenty-four matches being completed on the same day. This was despite one of the wettest Mays on record and it might have been different had the tournament started earlier than 9 June.

The group matches saw some exciting cricket and some surprises. An Allan Lamb century for England at The Oval saw a less enviable hundred achieved by a New Zealand player, Martin Snedden, who had the dubious honour of becoming the first bowler to concede 100 runs in an ODI innings. Snedden's analysis, though, came in 12 overs.

There was a welcome for Pakistan on the Welsh coast town of Swansea where they and Sri Lanka racked up the highest ODI match aggregate at that stage with 626 runs for 14 wickets with Pakistan winning by 50 runs. The Pakistan innings saw the first instance of four successive batsman passing fifty in a World Cup innings.

Two upsets also took place on the first two days of the tournament. In their first ever ODI, Zimbabwe defeated Australia at Trent Bridge by 13 runs, with future England coach Duncan Fletcher inspiring his side to victory with an unbeaten 69 before adding four for 42 with the ball. It would be their only World Cup victory until 1992, when they defended a modest total to beat England at Albury. Fletcher is still the only captain to score a fifty and take four wickets in a World Cup match.

The second needed an extra day at Old Trafford for the sensational first World Cup defeat for West Indies. That their defeat came against India was a surprise, as India had only managed one victory in two previous World Cup tournaments and that against East Africa. Yashpal Sharma's 89 for the victors took India to 262 for eight. Very much in it at 67 for two overnight, West Indies collapsed quickly the next day to 157 for nine. Roberts and Garner, with 37 apiece, added a record 71 and threatened, as in the 1975 match against Pakistan, to break the hearts of their opponents. Ultimately, Garner fell to Shastri and India had achieved a notable victory by 34 runs.

At Taunton, David Gower's 130 took England to an impressive 333 for eight and, despite an anonymous match for the local star, Botham, England won by 47 runs. Another Somerset player, Vic Marks, took England's first five-wicket haul in the World Cup finishing with five for 39 which remain England's best figures in the competition.

West Indies returned to winning ways against Australia with a two-day, 101-run victory at Headingley. Winston Davis's seven for 51 for the victors was, at that stage, the best bowling performance in the World Cup.

India's resurgence continued with a five wicket win over Zimbabwe at Leicester with Syed Kirmani becoming the first wicket-keeper to take five catches in a World Cup innings. Graeme Fowler started a four-match consecutive run of fifties – a record by an Englishman in the World Cup – as England beat Pakistan at Lord's by eight wickets.

After their encouraging start, India came a very distant second to Australia at Trent Bridge losing by 162 runs chasing 321. After a bright start and David Gower's unbeaten 92 at Edgbaston, England were beaten by New Zealand by two wickets with just one ball remaining.

India and West Indies met again at The Oval on 15 June, but a Viv Richards century took West Indies to 282 for nine after Clive Lloyd had won the toss. Despite 80 from Mohinder Amarnath, India's challenge petered out after Dilip Vengsarkar had to retire hurt and West Indies won comfortably by 66 runs.

Pakistan recovered from a precarious 43 for five at Headingley through captain Imran Khan's unbeaten 102 to reach 235 for seven which proved just enough to see them home by 11 runs. It was Pakistan's and the tournament's loss that Khan was unable to bowl during the competition due to injury.

Australia exacted revenge over Zimbabwe in the return match at Southampton but the Associate team still performed creditably only losing by 32 runs after chasing 273.

One of the most memorable World Cup matches took place at Tunbridge Wells, hosting its solitary ODI to date. Electing to bat first, India were reduced to nine for four with the cream of the batting removed as Kapil Dev strode out. The score soon became 17 for five but Kapil remained. A platform was achieved through a partnership of 60 with Roger Binny but, once again, a first-ever semi-final spot was in jeopardy as the seventh wicket fell at 78.

Aided by partnerships of 62 with Madan Lal and an unbeaten 126 with Kirmani, Kapil launched a furious but sensible assault and ended up with 175 not out from India's 266 for eight. Kapil's innings included six sixes and 16 fours from just 138 balls and was at that stage the highest ODI innings and certainly one of the most important.

Still Zimbabwe made a game challenge through Kevin Curran's 73 but ultimately India came through by 31 runs and kept their hopes of a semi-final space alive.

Every side won at least one match during this tournament and Sri Lanka landed theirs with a tense win at Derby over New Zealand. Ashantha de Mel became the second bowler – and last to date – after Gary Gilmour in 1975 to take five wickets in successive World Cup matches. On the larger grounds on the same day as the Derby and Tunbridge Wells games, England comfortably completed a seven-wicket win over Pakistan which took them into the semi-finals whilst West Indies made light work of a stiffer victory target of 274 against Australia at Lord's.

Pakistan's match against New Zealand at Trent Bridge found the Asian side needing not only to beat their opponents but to score well enough to take their run rate above New Zealand's. They succeeded in both scoring 261 for three with a century, after four near misses since 1975, from Zaheer Abbas and a further, unbeaten 79 from Imran and in a tight finish, held on by 11 runs after New Zealand's ninth-wicket pair of Jeremy Coney and John Bracewell had threatened to spoil the show. It was the first time that New Zealand had failed to reach the semi-finals.

After a topsy-turvy tournament, Australia could have reached the semi-finals had they beaten India at Chelmsford. They had their chances needing 248 but a middle-order collapse to the medium pacers of Madan Lal and Binny saw them finish well short at 129 all out, thus ensuring India's first-ever World Cup semi-final.

With West Indies very easily defeating Zimbabwe by ten wickets after an unbeaten opening stand of 172 between Haynes and Faoud Bacchus, the semi-final line up was confirmed with England playing India at Old Trafford and West Indies, as in 1979, facing Pakistan again and again at The Oval.

The Old Trafford match saw England start quite reasonably through Fowler and Tavare but a sluggish pitch suited the slower and medium-paced bowlers of Binny, Kirti Azad and Amarnath and runs dried up whilst wickets regularly went down. Having reached 100 with only two down, England only managed 213 from their full quota of overs due to a late flourish from Graham Dilley.

Although the openers of Gavaskar and Srikkanth had gone by the time the total had just reached 50, fine contributions from Man of the Match Amarnath, Yashpal Sharma and Sandeep Patil ensured that it was India, who during this competition beat Test playing opposition for the first time in the three World Cups, reached the Lord's final at the expense of the hosts.

In a repeat of one of the 1979 semi-finals between West Indies and Pakistan, it was once again West Indies who prevailed and this time by the more comfortable margin of eight wickets with 11.2 overs remaining. The Richards and Larry Gomes undefeated partnership of 132 ensured that the defending champions reached their third consecutive World Cup final and had lost only two wickets in their preceding two matches in achieving it. India's defeat of England had meant that the same two teams of 1979 would not contest the third final.

A crowd of just over 24,600 watched the Lord's final between two-time champions, West Indies, and India. The defending champions were undoubtedly the favourites, but a remarkable day unfolded in front of the packed audience. After Gavaskar's early dismissal, the most fluent batting – and indeed highest score of the day – came from the aggressive Srikkanth in partnership with the more resolute Amarnath.

India, though, were never in control and wickets tumbled regularly and even a 22-run, last- wicket partnership which took the score up to only 183 did not fill those watching and participating with a conviction that a shock might be in store.

Despite Greenidge's third early final dismissal, an imperious Richards innings saw the fifty reached without further loss. However, a mistimed hook off Madan Lal and a fine running catch by Kapil Dev cut his innings short in comparative infancy. It opened perhaps surprising floodgates with the same medium-pacers and Madan Lal wreaking havoc with the West Indian middle order and a platform of 50 for one had become 76 for six.

Sensible batting from wicket-keeper Jeff Dujon and tearaway fast bowler Malcolm Marshall forged a partnership to the point where West Indies were reaching the stage where a third victory was looking possible. Man of the Match Mohinder Amarnath ensured that, with figures of three for 12 in seven overs, it was not to be and remarkable and never-to-be-forgotten scenes occurred when Amarnath's dismissal of Michael Holding meant that the formidable champions of 1975 and 1983 gave way to the unfancied side at the beginning of the competition.

1983 MISCELLANY

- All three finals which West Indies reached in World Cup tournaments have been at Lord's.
- New Zealand's Martin Snedden became the first bowler to concede 100 runs in an ODI. The only others in World Cup history are Jason Holder (10-2-104-1) for West Indies vs South Africa at Sydney in 2015 and Afghanistan's Dawlat Zadran (10-1-101-2) vs Australia at Perth in 2015. Snedden bowled 12 overs in 1983.
- The Pakistan and New Zealand game at Edgbaston saw the first-ever instance in an ODI of the first three wickets falling before a run had been scored. The same has now happened on two further occasions.
- After beating Australia at Trent Bridge, Zimbabwe would lose their next eighteen World Cup matches.
- Zimbabwe became the first non-Test playing team to win their first full ODI.

- Mohinder Amarnath became the first of three cricketers to win a semi-final and final Man of the Match award in the same competition. Aravinda de Silva in 1996 and Shane Warne in 1999 achieved the same feat. Viv Richards won a semi-final award in 1983 and the final award in 1979.
- Headingley remains the ground with most performances of five wickets in an innings in the World Cup with five. All were achieved in the 1975 and 1983 tournaments but not in 1979 or 1999.
- The 1983 final remains the only one without an individual fifty.

1983 STATISTICS

HIGHEST TOTALS	
338 for 5 in 60 overs	Pakistan vs. Sri Lanka at Swansea
333 for 9 in 60 overs	England vs. Sri Lanka at Taunton
322 for 6 in 60 overs	England vs. New Zealand at The Oval
320 for 9 in 60 overs	Australia vs. India at Nottingham

LOWEST COMPLETED TOTALS	
129 in 38.2 overs	Australia vs. India at Chelmsford
136 in 50.4 overs	Sri Lanka vs. England at Leeds
140 in 52 overs	West Indies vs. India at Lord's

HIGHEST MATCH AGGREGATES	
626 for 14 wickets	Pakistan (338-5) vs. Sri Lanka (288-9) at Swansea
619 for 19 wickets	England (333-9) vs. Sri Lanka (286) at Taunton
549 for 9 wickets	Australia (273-6) vs. West Indies (276-3) at Lord's
538 for 16 wickets	England (322-6) vs. New Zealand (216) at The Oval

LOWEST MATCH AGGEGATES WITH RESULT	
273 for 11 wickets	Sri Lanka (136) vs. England (137-1) at Leeds
312 for 15 wickets	Zimbabwe (155) vs. India (157-5) at Leicester
323 for 20 wickets	India (183) vs. West Indies (140) at Lord's

BIGGEST VICTORY MARGINS	
162 runs	Australia (320-9) vs. India (158) at Nottingham
118 runs	India (247) vs. Australia (129) at Chelmsford
106 runs	England (322-6) vs. New Zealand (216) at The Oval
101 runs	West Indies (252-9) vs. Australia (151) at Leeds
10 wickets	West Indies (172-0) vs. Zimbabwe (171) at Birmingham
9 wickets	England (137-1) vs. Sri Lanka (136) at Leeds

LOWEST VICTORY MARGINS	
11 runs	Pakistan (235-7) vs. Sri Lanka (224) at Leeds
11 runs	Pakistan (261-3) vs. New Zealand (250) at Nottingham
13 runs	Zimbabwe (239-6) vs. Australia (226-7) at Nottingham
2 wickets	New Zealand (238-8) vs. England (234) at Birmingham
3 wickets	Sri Lanka (184-7) vs. New Zealand (181) at Derby

LEADING RUN SCORERS	
384 (average 76.80)	David Gower (England)
367 (average 73.40)	Viv Richards (West Indies)
360 (average 72.00)	Graeme Fowler (England)

HIGHEST SCORES		
175*	Kapil Dev	India vs. Zimbabwe at Tunbridge Wells
130	David Gower	England vs. Sri Lanka at Taunton
119	Viv Richards	West Indies vs. India at The Oval
110	Trevor Chappell	Australia vs. India at Nottingham

CENTURIES
Eight

LEADING WICKET TAKERS	
18 (average 18.67)	Roger Binny (India)
17 (average 15.59)	Ashantha de Mel (Sri Lanka)
17 (average 16.76)	Madan Lal (India)

BEST BOWLING PERFORMANCES

10.3-0-51-7	Winston Davis	West Indies vs. Australia at Leeds
11.5-3-39-6	Ken MacLeay	Australia vs. India at Nottingham
10.1-4-25-5	Richard Hadlee	New Zealand vs. Sri Lanka at Bristol

FIVE WICKETS IN AN INNINGS
Eight

HIGHEST PARTNERSHIPS IN EACH WICKET

1	172*	Desmond Haynes & Faoud Bacchus	WI vs. Zim	Birmingham
2	144	Trevor Chappell & Kim Hughes	Aus. vs. Ind	Nottingham
3	195*	Gordon Greenidge & Larry Gomes	WI vs. Zim.	Worcester
4	147*	Zaheer Abbas & Imran Khan	Pak. vs. NZ	Nottingham
5	92	David Houghton & Duncan Fletcher	Zim. vs. WI	Worcester
6	144	Imran Khan & Shahid Mahboob	Pak. vs. SL	Leeds
7	75*	Duncan Fletcher & Iain Butchart	Zim. vs. Aus.	Nottingham
8	62	Kapil Dev & Madan Lal	Ind. vs. Zim.	Tunbridge Wells
9	126*	Kapil Dev & Syed Kirmani	Ind. vs. Zim.	Tunbridge Wells
10	71	Andy Roberts & Joel Garner	WI vs. Ind	Manchester

1987

After the 1983 final, the ICC had sought tenders from nations interested in hosting the fourth World Cup. Ultimately, it became a joint venture between India and Pakistan co-hosting an event which again contained twenty-seven matches but over twenty-one venues (including two Hyderabads) in both countries. Matches would consist of fifty overs per side as the light could not be relied upon to allow a finish as late as had been possible in England.

Despite the vast distances and the potential for travelling difficulties, the first World Cup tournament outside England was considered a great success. Sri Lanka had, at times, a demanding travelling schedule whilst the hosts played all their games in their own countries. The eight teams – the same from 1983 – would play for the Reliance Cup and would again be divided into two groups.

Group A contained India, Australia, New Zealand and Zimbabwe whilst Group B saw Pakistan, England, West Indies and Sri Lanka contest the group. There was excitement from the word go.

After a maiden Javed Miandad World Cup century in his fourth tournament, Pakistan made the ideal start, holding off Sri Lanka in Hyderabad (Pakistan), by 15 runs. India seemed on course to start with an opening victory in Madras against Australia, but an extraordinary match went to the final over.

A Geoff Marsh century had taken Australia to 268 for six in their 50 overs only for two runs to be added at the interval after a fairly obvious Dean Jones six, initially signalled as four, was duly corrected. It seemed to make little difference as Sunil Gavaskar, Krishnamachari Srikkanth and Navjot Sidhu, playing in his first ODI, appeared to have made light work of the target.

Wickets, though, fell and Steve Waugh, who would regularly bowl effectively at the end of the innings, had six runs to defend whilst India had only their last wicket pair of Maninder Singh and wicket-keeper, Kiran More. The previous year, Maninder had been the last man dismissed to secure only the second Tied Test and he was again last out in this match on the same ground, his stumps spread-eagled by Waugh's fifth ball of the over. This time, India were one short and had lost the first match in their defence in front of a crowd which had become more subdued as Indian wickets fell.

England had arrived with a specialist in tropical diseases and a microwave but could do little about a very early departure from their hotel near Lahore for their match against West Indies at Gujranwala. After being put in, the West Indian total of 243 for seven looked to be sufficient until a charge from Allan Lamb saw England scramble home by three wickets with three balls remaining. Courtney Walsh, suffering in the latter stages with direction and no-balls, conceded 31 runs in two overs as England scored their first World Cup success against the two-time champions.

Another remarkable game took place in Hyderabad (India) between New Zealand and Zimbabwe. After reaching 242 for seven, there seemed little chance of a close finish when Zimbabwe lost their seventh wicket at 104. Their captain, Dave Houghton, found support with Iain Butchart and the pair added 117 before Houghton's 136-ball, boundary-laden 142 took Zimbabwe to within touching distance of their total. They fell short by just three runs when Butchart was run out for 54 with just two balls remaining.

Zimbabwe fared less well against Australia at Madras whilst at Rawalpindi, England suffered a bad collapse to Pakistan and lost the match by 18 runs when they might reasonably have expected to have won. A slightly strained match saw a few words exchanged after Miandad had been dismissed lbw to de Freitas – only his fourth such occasion in an ODI in Pakistan – and after a sluggish start, England had reached a more dominant position when late wickets handed the initiative to the hosts.

Viv Richards became the World Cup's highest scorer with 181 at Karachi against Sri Lanka in an easy 191-run win. Having entered on a hat-trick, he added 182 with Desmond Haynes (who made his own century). Richards's innings remains the highest World Cup score by a captain and it was the first occasion of two centurions in a World Cup innings.

India achieved their first points with a narrow win over New Zealand at Bangalore after a poor start. Sidhu (75), Kapil Dev (72 not out) and More (42 not out) helped India to 252 for seven before New Zealand fell short at 236 for eight after contributions from Snedden, who opened the batting and bowling regularly during the tournament, Ken Rutherford and Andrew Jones.

Pakistan overcame West Indies in Lahore by one wicket in a thrilling match from the last ball. After his difficult finish to the match against England, Walsh had sportingly resisted running out Saleem Jaffer for backing up too far before delivering the final ball.

England's journey to the North West Frontier town of Peshawar resulted in a 108-run victory over Sri Lanka after scoring 296 for four and using nine bowlers in restricting Sri Lanka to 158 for eight. The target was revised after a weather delay during the Sri Lankan innings.

Rain in Indore reduced the Australia and New Zealand game to a 30-over per side and New Zealand, having reached the last over requiring seven to win with four wickets intact, managed to lose by three runs.

England lost again to Pakistan in Karachi in a game where the former promised more through a Bill Athey and Mike Gatting partnership of 135 but their eventual total of 244 for nine proved insufficient as a century from Ramiz Raja and 88 from Salim Malik led to a seven-wicket victory for Pakistan thereby reaching the semi-finals.

West Indies regained some ground with a 25-run win over Sri Lanka at Kanpur, but it was nonetheless not one of the most convincing displays from the former champions. After their opening game at Madras, India enjoyed an easier ride with a 56-run win over Australia with Maninder Singh and Azharuddin taking three wickets each as India successfully defended 289 at Delhi.

After their two defeats to Pakistan, England's match at Jaipur against West Indies became important if they wished to seal a semi-final berth. Having achieved their first World Cup victory over West Indies earlier in the tournament, Gooch's 92 and a good helping of extras saw England to 269 for five.

Richie Richardson and Richards kept West Indies very much in contention but, with each of England's five bowlers picking up wickets, the West Indian challenge again ended leaving England with a vital 34-run victory.

Although India beat Zimbabwe easily enough at Ahmedabad, run rate was becoming an important factor in Group A establishing which side qualified top and despite their seven-wicket success, they still found themselves marginally behind Australia's scoring rate.

That said, Australia next played New Zealand at Chandigarh and Geoff Marsh's second century of the competition and 56 from Dean Jones saw Australia reach 150 for only one wicket. However, the 200 was reached in the 45th over and it needed a rare expensive over from Ewen Chatfield for Australia to reach 251 for eight.

New Zealand enjoyed a decent start but, with Martin Crowe being unfortunately run out and other batsmen making starts but no-one going further than opener Wright's 61, they fell 17 runs short.

England reached their fourth successive World Cup semi-final with an eight-wicket victory over Sri Lanka at Pune. Roy Dias's 80 allowed Sri Lanka to reach 218 for 7 but with scores of more than 40 by Gooch, Tim Robinson, Athey and Gatting, the target was achieved with 8.4 overs remaining.

After an Australian win over Zimbabwe by 70 runs at Cuttack, India found themselves requiring 224 in 42.2 overs against New Zealand at Nagpur to win the group. His undefeated 36 at Lord's in 1975 a long-distant memory, Gavaskar (103 not out in 88 balls) and Srikkanth (75 in 58 balls) launched such an assault on all the bowlers that victory was achieved after only 32.1 overs. The match was also memorable for the first World Cup hat-trick taken by Chetan Sharma who bowled all of his victims, Rutherford, Ian Smith and Chatfield.

Despite Pakistan's defeat to West Indies at Karachi, the hosts still qualified top of Group B and for the first time, West Indies failed to reach the semi-finals. During this match, Viv Richards became the first player to score 1000 World Cup runs. The semi-finals would be Pakistan against Australia at Lahore and India would take on England at Bombay. The general feeling and hope was that the hosts would meet each other for the first time in the World Cup in the final but, on the day, the other sides had different ideas.

Australia, enjoying a slight renaissance after being unfancied at the start of the tournament, batted first in Lahore and had useful contributions all the way down the order but none higher than David Boon's 65. Extras again featured prominently. Boon's innings was ended by substitute wicket-keeper Miandad's stumping after an injury to the named keeper, Salim Yousuf. A misfiring Saleem Jaffer conceded 18 runs in the last over of the innings to allow Australia to reach 267 for eight.

Miandad and Imran fashioned a recovery after the first three Pakistani wickets had fallen for 38 but, with the asking rate reaching almost eight an over, the chase was never straightforward. Craig McDermott's five for 44, aided by four catches by wicket-keeper Greg Dyer finished off Pakistan's innings at 249. Pakistan, firm contenders at the start of the tournament, lost their third successive semi-final and the first co-host had been eliminated.

In Bombay, Kapil Dev inserted England and watched Gooch famously sweep his way to 115 as England posted 254 for six. Gavaskar bowed out of international cricket for just four and India were never completely in the chase. Even though India passed 200 with five wickets down, Eddie Hemmings's four quick wickets snuffed out any potential tail-end resistance as the last five wickets fell for just 15 runs and ensured that the final which the subcontinent wanted was not to be. It would be between the two oldest adversaries, England and Australia.

Eden Gardens in Calcutta, one of the largest stadia in world cricket, hosted a memorable final. On winning the toss, Australia enjoyed a good start with 52 in the first ten overs. Attritional play through the middle stages was backed up by a late burst of 73 in the final overs which took Australia to 253 for five with the top score being Boon's 75. The first six batsmen all reached double figures and only Steve Waugh, who came in late on and was unbeaten with five at the end, failed to do so. Spinners Hemmings and Emburey stemmed the flow of runs after the initial burst from de Freitas and Gladstone Small.

England's start was a poor one with Robinson dismissed for a duck. Solid partnerships of 65 and 69 involving Gooch, Athey and Gatting gave England hope but Gatting's dismissal to a reverse sweep from the first ball of opposing captain Allan Border's spell helped to turn the tide towards Australia.

There were still useful performances from Lamb and the tail-enders but an asking rate of 7.5 runs per over from the last ten overs proved tough and, despite de Freitas raising England's hopes with 14 in McDermott's ninth over, it was Australia who prevailed by just seven runs in securing their first World Cup triumph. For England, it was another occasion of not being quite close enough and the match remains the closest final in terms of runs. For the fourth World Cup final, the side batting first had won.

1987 MISCELLANY

- There have been two one-run results in World Cup history and India have been the losers on both occasions to Australia. After their 1987 defeat at Madras, the same happened to them at Brisbane in 1992.
- Derek Pringle joined his father, Don, who played for East Africa in 1975, as the first father and son to both appear in the World Cup.
- Using nine bowlers in an innings has occurred only twice in World Cup matches. After the England and Sri Lanka game in Peshawar, New Zealand used the same number against Pakistan at Christchurch in 1992.
- Allan Border's 2 for 38 is the best bowling by a captain in a World Cup final.
- Border remains the only captain to dismiss the opposition captain in a World Cup final.
- Ewen Chatfield's record-breaking sequence of seven innings in twelve matches without being out stretching back to 1979 and three World Cups, ended ignominiously in his last World Cup innings, with his first-ball dismissal at Nagpur giving Chetan Sharma the World Cup's first hat-trick.

1987 STATISTICS

HIGHEST TOTALS	
360 for 4 in 50 overs	West Indies vs. Sri Lanka at Karachi
297 for 7 in 50 overs	Pakistan vs. Sri Lanka at Faisalabad
296 for 4 in 50 overs	England vs. Sri Lanka at Peshawar
289 for 6 in 50 overs	India vs. Australia at Delhi

LOWEST TOTALS	
135 in 44.2 overs	Zimbabwe vs. India at Bombay
139 in 42.4 overs	Zimbabwe vs. Australia at Madras

HIGHEST MATCH AGGREGATES	
539 for 16 wickets	Australia (270-6) vs. India (269) at Madras
529 for 8 wickets	West Indies (360-4) vs. Sri Lanka (169-4) at Karachi
522 for 16 wickets	India (289-6) vs. Australia (233) at Delhi
519 for 16 wickets	Pakistan (267-6) vs. Sri Lanka (252) at Hyderabad

LOWEST MATCH AGGREGATES WITH RESULT	
271 for 12 wickets	Zimbabwe (135) vs. India (136-2) at Bombay
374 for 19 wickets	Australia (235-9) vs. Zimbabwe (139) at Madras
385 for 10 wickets	Zimbabwe (191-7) vs. India (194-3) at Ahmedabad

BIGGEST VICTORY MARGINS	
191 runs	West Indies (360-4) vs. Sri Lanka (169-4) at Karachi
113 runs	Pakistan (297-7) vs. Sri Lanka (184-8) at Faisalabad
108 runs	England (296-4) vs. Sri Lanka (158-8) at Peshawar
9 wickets	India (224-1) vs. New Zealand (221-9) at Nagpur

LOWEST VICTORY MARGINS	
1 run	Australia (270-6) vs. India (269) at Madras
3 runs	Australia (199-4) vs. New Zealand (196-9) at Indore
3 runs	New Zealand (242-7) vs. Zimbabwe (239) at Hyderabad
7 runs	Australia (253-5) vs. England (246-8) at Calcutta
1 wicket	Pakistan (217-9) vs. West Indies (216) at Lahore
2 wickets	England (246-8) vs. West Indies (243-7) at Gujranwala

LEADING RUN SCORERS	
471 (average 58.88)	Graham Gooch (England)
447 (average 55.88)	David Boon (Australia)
428 (average 61.14)	Geoff Marsh (Australia)

HIGHEST SCORES

181	Viv Richards	West Indies vs. Sri Lanka at Karachi
142	David Houghton	Zimbabwe vs. New Zealand at Hyderabad
126*	Geoff Marsh	Australia vs. New Zealand at Chandigarh
115	Graham Gooch	England vs. India at Bombay
113	Ramiz Raja	Pakistan vs. England at Karachi

CENTURIES

Eleven

LEADING WICKET TAKERS

18 (average 18.94)	Craig McDermott (Australia)
17 (average 13.06)	Imran Khan (Pakistan)

BEST BOWLING PERFORMANCES

10-0-44-5	Craig McDermott	Australia vs. Pakistan at Lahore
8-1-19-4	Manoj Prabhakar	India vs. Zimbabwe at Bombay

FIVE WICKETS IN AN INNINGS

One

HIGHEST PARTNERSHIPS IN EACH WICKET

1	136	Kris Srikkanth & Sunil Gavaskar	Ind. vs. NZ	Nagpur
2	167	Ramiz Raja & Salim Malik	Pak. vs. Eng	Karachi
3	182	Desmond Haynes & Viv Richards	WI vs. SL	Karachi
4	116	Viv Richards & Gus Logie	WI vs. SL	Karachi
5	83	Jeff Dujon & Gus Logie	WI vs. Eng	Gujranwala
6	73	Imran Khan & Saleem Yousuf	Pak. vs. WI	Lahore
7	46*	Jeff Crowe & Ian Smith	NZ vs. Zim	Calcutta
8	117	David Houghton & Iain Butchart	Zim. vs. NZ	Hyderabad
9	39	Martin Snedden & Willie Watson	NZ vs. Ind.	Nagpur
10	36	Andy Pycroft & Malcolm Jarvis	Zim. vs. Ind.	Bombay

1992

After Australia's 1987 World Cup win, New Zealand and Australia agreed to tender for the next World Cup in 1992. When it was formally announced that the event would be held in Australasia, there would be changes and thirty-nine matches would be played with twenty-five in Australia and fourteen in New Zealand.

All Test nations would be represented and after their re-admission to the Test scene, South Africa was also included just four months before the event started. Having won the 1990 ICC Trophy, Zimbabwe also retained their place so the nine countries participating was the most at that point in any one World Cup event.

It was also the first event played in colour clothing, under floodlights and with a white ball. All matches would be over 50 overs per innings. The official title was The Benson and Hedges World Cup and there would be just the one group with each team playing each other once before the top four took part in the semi-finals.

A rain rule was introduced which essentially deducted the least productive overs in the first innings from those in the second. Spare days could not be built into the tournament and the rain rule provided some unsatisfactory finishes.

Australia started as favourites but their first match against co-hosts New Zealand in Auckland provided a slight shock with a 37-run defeat. After John Wright's dismissal to the first legitimate ball of the tournament – the third – it was not just captain Martin Crowe's unbeaten 100 which caught the eye but New Zealand's interesting and different tactics in opening the bowling with off-spinner, Dipak Patel, throughout the tournament but also using slow-medium bowlers to take the pace off the ball. It is fair to say that their ideas worked handsomely.

South Africa slotted in comfortably and impressively. They not only had a very able team and a spearhead fast bowler in Allan Donald but were led by Kepler Wessels, who had represented Australia in the 1983 World Cup. When they too beat Australia at Sydney by nine wickets to inflict the second defeat in as many matches, not everything was looking rosy for the co-hosts.

Zimbabwe started with a high-scoring defeat at New Plymouth, hosting its only international match, against Sri Lanka with Andy Flower marking his ODI debut with an unbeaten 115 in his side's 312 for four. It did not prove quite enough with Sri Lanka winning with four balls remaining.

A somewhat odd match at Melbourne saw West Indies beat Pakistan by ten wickets in a match which produced 441 runs for the loss of just two wickets. Brian Lara was forced to retire hurt after scoring 88 at 175 in the West Indian innings but Haynes and Richardson saw their side home at 221-0 with 3.1 overs left.

After England had triumphed for the third successive time in the World Cup against West Indies in another match at Melbourne, rain restricted Mackay's only international match to just two balls between India and Sri Lanka.

New Zealand's different policy was paying dividends with further victories over Sri Lanka at Hamilton and South Africa at Auckland but at Brisbane Australia finally managed their first victory against India. Like Madras in 1987, it was by just one run and the rain rule reduced India's target by just two runs with three fewer overs. Venkatapathy Raju was the last batsman dismissed.

An extraordinary game at Adelaide saw Pakistan inserted by England and found themselves languishing at 47 for eight. Wasim Haider and Mushtaq Ahmed, at numbers nine and ten, were two of just three batsmen to reach double figures and helped Pakistan reach 74. Derek Pringle was the most successful bowler with three for eight. It was Pakistan's lowest ODI total at that stage.

Rain then again disrupted another match and, after the tournament rules had been applied twice to allow for a further delay, England's target was 64 from 16 overs but ultimately, at 24 for one after eight overs, the match was abandoned denying England a likely victory.

The first World Cup meeting between India and Pakistan finally took place at Sydney. Although India only managed 216 for seven,

18-year-old Sachin Tendulkar made his maiden World Cup fifty. The match was remembered for a spat between Indian wicket-keeper, Kiran More, and Javed Miandad and which the managers of the respective sides were asked to sort out. The umpires' reports had been unable to comment on what was said as it was said in the vernacular. Despite their low score, India prevailed comfortably by 43 runs.

After losses to New Zealand and Sri Lanka, South Africa returned to form with a 64-run win against West Indies at Christchurch. England added to Australia's woes by bowling them out for 171 at Sydney and winning handsomely by eight wickets. Ian Botham became only the second player to make 50 and take four wickets in a World Cup match and his is still England's best all-round performance.

Australia were pleased to make amends and record victory over Sri Lanka at Adelaide whilst New Zealand's defeat of West Indies at Auckland was their fifth successive victory in the competition. The West Indian victory over India was memorable for its being the first where a side successfully pursued a rain-restricted target.

South Africa beat their neighbours Zimbabwe in Canberra and the defeated side included the former South African Test off-spinner, Egyptian-born John Traicos. He would later debut for the Zimbabwean Test team after the World Cup.

New Zealand went from strength to strength, winning their sixth and seventh successive matches against India and England, the latter match confirming New Zealand as winners of the group with England second and both assured of semi-final spaces. This winning streak would be New Zealand's best in the World Cup until they bettered it with eight consecutive wins in 2015.

Australia managed to beat the winless Zimbabwe in Hobart which kept the hosts mathematically in contention for a semi-final spot. South Africa's defeat of India in Adelaide assured them of their position in the knock-out stages of the tournament.

Pakistan, performing far better than at the start of the tournament, beat Australia and Sri Lanka and then faced the undefeated New Zealand in Christchurch. It turned out that the two sides would meet in the semi-final but, in the unknown dress rehearsal, Pakistan inflicted the co-host's first defeat with a comfortable seven-wicket victory and thereby reached the semi-final stage.

Pakistan's entrance to the last four was only confirmed at the end of the Australia and West Indies match. Australia knew that their playing interest in the competition ended with the news that Pakistan had beaten New Zealand, yet Pakistan only knew that their place was secure when West Indies, after a reasonable chance to beat Australia, failed to do so.

Although there was little riding on the England and Zimbabwe match in Albury, there was a surprise nine-run win for Zimbabwe after making just 134. It ended their drought of eighteen consecutive World Cup defeats dating back to after their first-ever match in 1983 when they defeated Australia.

The semi-finals saw the re-match between New Zealand and Pakistan at Auckland whilst England reached their fifth successive World Cup semi-final and would play South Africa at Sydney.

Martin Crowe's impressive performance as captain continued with the bat as he made 91 at Auckland and, with 50 from Ken Rutherford, New Zealand ended on 262 for seven. Unfortunately for New Zealand, Crowe injured himself, so Wright captained during the Pakistani innings. All seemed to be set fair as the Pakistani innings ended up in the doldrums and with 15 overs left, they needed 123 runs.

Javed Miandad, in his fifth World Cup, and an up-and-coming batsman, Inzamam-ul-Haq, who had been unwell the night before, added 87 in 10 overs before Inzamam, run out for the fourth time in his previous five innings, was dismissed for 60 which included one six and seven fours in just 37 balls. Miandad's unbeaten 57 meant that Pakistan had beaten the previously unbeaten New Zealand twice in four days, putting them out again at the semi-final stage of another World Cup.

There was a less satisfactory ending to the Sydney match where rain interfered at an inappropriate time. After England had finished with 252 for six in just forty-five overs due to a dilatory over rate, all eight South African batsman who came in reached double figures but, with the run rate increasing, South Africa gave themselves a chance until the rains came.

Twelve minutes were lost to rain and South Africa's target was reduced from 22 in 13 balls to 22 in seven and ultimately the big scoreboard announced that, when the South African batsmen returned, their target was 21 in one ball and England were through to their third final.

England therefore met Pakistan in front of over 87,000 spectators – considerably more than the other four games played at the ground – at

Melbourne. Pakistan came into the match having prospered in the latter matches and after winning the toss, Imran chose to bat.

The wickets of Ramiz Raja and Aamir Sohail, Pakistan's tournament centurions, fell quickly and at the halfway point, Pakistan had reached just 70 but, after a period of attrition, Imran and Miandad opened up to add 139 in 31 overs before Miandad was another World Cup final victim of a reverse sweep. Vital contributions of 42 from Inzamam and 33 from Wasim Akram, both at better than a run a ball, saw Pakistan close on 249 for six. Pringle's miserly three for 22 remains England's best in a World Cup final.

England too started badly with Botham, who had been used as opener throughout the tournament, dismissed without scoring and Alec Stewart also out at 21. Despite a resurgence through Neil Fairbrother and Allan Lamb after the fourth wicket had fallen at 69, two remarkable and successive deliveries from Akram to dismiss Lamb and Chris Lewis pretty much put paid to another England challenge.

Despite Fairbrother's 63 and the last four batsmen all reaching double figures, the chase was always just beyond England's scope and, fittingly, it was Imran who sealed Pakistan's first World Cup with a 22-run victory when he dismissed Richard Illingworth. The proceeds of the win would help towards Imran's ambition for a cancer hospital in Lahore in memory of his mother.

Whilst Pakistan have not to date added to this World Cup success, England's fortunes since this 1992 defeat have plummeted and they have not reached a semi-final in the ensuing six tournaments.

The fifth World Cup final, like the previous four, had been won by the side batting first.

1992 MISCELLANY

- Kepler Wessels became the first of four players to represent two countries at the World Cup. Anderson Cummins (West Indies & Canada), Eoin Morgan and Ed Joyce (both Ireland and England) are the others.
- Andy Flower is the only batsman to score a century on ODI debut in a World Cup match.

- India and Pakistan's first World Cup match was the first of six such contested between the teams. India have won all six.
- Pakistan's 74 was the lowest total in a World Cup between two Test playing countries until Bangladesh were dismissed for 58 against West Indies at Dhaka in 2011.
- Zimbabwe's 134 all out against England at Albury is the lowest completed total to be successfully defended in the World Cup.
- 1992 is the only World Cup tournament where no bowler took five wickets in an innings.
- The West Indies and Pakistan match at Melbourne remains the World Cup match to be completed with the fewest wickets to fall, in this case two.

1992 STATISTICS

HIGHEST TOTALS	
313 for 7 in 49.2 overs	Sri Lanka vs. Zimbabwe at New Plymouth
312 for 4 in 50 overs	Zimbabwe vs. Sri Lanka at New Plymouth
280 for 6 in 50 overs	England vs. Sri Lanka in Ballarat

LOWEST COMPLETED TOTALS	
74 in 40.2 overs	Pakistan vs. England at Adelaide
125 in 49.1 overs	England vs. Zimbabwe at Albury
134 in 46.1 overs	Zimbabwe vs. England at Albury
136 in 38.4 overs	West Indies vs. South Africa at Christchurch
137 in 41.4 overs	Zimbabwe vs. Australia at Hobart

HIGHEST MATCH AGGREGATES	
625 for 11 wickets	Sri Lanka (313-7) vs. Zimbabwe (312-4) at New Plymouth
526 for 13 wickets	New Zealand (262-7) vs. Pakistan (264-6) at Auckland

LOWEST MATCH AGGREGATES WITH RESULT	
259 for 20 wickets	Zimbabwe (134) vs. England (125) at Albury
267 for 10 wickets	New Zealand (162-3) vs. Zimbabwe (105-7) at Napier

BIGGEST VICTORY MARGINS	
128 runs	Australia (265-6) vs. Zimbabwe (137) at Hobart
106 runs	England (280-6) vs. Sri Lanka (174) at Ballarat
10 wickets	West Indies (221-0) vs. Pakistan (220-2) at Melbourne
9 wickets	South Africa (171-1) vs. Australia (170-9) at Sydney

LOWEST VICTORY MARGINS	
1 run	Australia (237-9) vs. India (234) at Brisbane
9 runs	England (236-9) vs. India (227) at Perth
9 runs	Zimbabwe (134) vs. England (125) at Albury
3 wickets	England (226-7) vs. South Africa (236-4) at Melbourne
3 wickets	Sri Lanka (198-7) vs. South Africa (195) at Wellington
3 wickets	Sri Lanka (313-7) vs. Zimbabwe (312-4) at New Plymouth

LEADING RUN SCORERS	
456 (average 114.00)	Martin Crowe (New Zealand)
437 (average 62.43)	Javed Miandad (Pakistan)
410 (average 68.33)	Peter Kirsten (South Africa)

HIGHEST SCORES		
119*	Ramiz Raja	Pakistan vs. New Zealand at Christchurch
115*	Andy Flower	Zimbabwe vs. Sri Lanka at New Plymouth
114	Aamer Sohail	Pakistan vs. Zimbabwe at Hobart
110	Phil Simmons	West Indies vs. Sri Lanka at Berri

CENTURIES
Eight

LEADING WICKET TAKERS	
18 (average 18.78)	Wasim Akram (Pakistan)
16 (average 19.13)	Ian Botham (England)
16 (average 19.44)	Mushtaq Ahmed (Pakistan)
16 (average 21.38)	Chris Harris (New Zealand)

BEST BOWLING PERFORMANCES

8-4-11-4	Meyrick Pringle	South Africa vs. West Indies at Christchurch
10-4-21-4	Eddo Brandes	Zimbabwe vs. England at Albury
8-0-30-4	Chris Lewis	England vs. Sri Lanka at Ballarat

FIVE WICKETS IN AN INNINGS

Zero

HIGHEST PARTNERSHIPS FOR EACH WICKET

1	175*	Desmond Haynes & Brian Lara	WI vs. Pak.	Melbourne
2	127	Mohammad Azharuddin & Sachin Tendulkar	Ind. vs. NZ	Dunedin
3	145	Aamer Sohail & Javed Miandad	Pak. vs. Zim	Hobart
4	118	Martin Crowe & Ken Rutherford	NZ vs. Aus	Auckland
5	145*	Andy Flower & Andy Waller	Zim. vs. SL	New Plymouth
6	83*	Keith Arthurton & Carl Hooper	WI vs. Ind	Wellington
7	46	Gus Logie & Desmond Haynes	WI vs. SA	Christchurch
8	33	Graeme Labrooy & Champaka Ramanayake	SL vs. Eng.	Ballarat
9	44	Gavin Larsen & Danny Morrison	NZ vs. Pak.	Christchurch
10	28*	Ruwan Kalpage & Pramodya Wickramasinghe	SL vs. WI	Berri

1996

It was felt that the World Cup would return to England after competitions in Asia in 1987 and Australasia in 1992 but a late night and long, at times, rancorous meeting at Lord's led to an eventual decision that the competition be hosted again in the subcontinent. Sri Lanka would also be included in the scheduling and it was agreed that England would stage the 1999 World Cup.

If the 1987 edition in India and Pakistan had been deemed a success, the 1996 version hit trouble and not everything went according to plan. A bomb in Colombo shortly before the start of the tournament led to Australia and West Indies pulling out of matches in the Sri Lankan capital and after further lengthy meetings, the games and points were awarded to Sri Lanka. Such was the nature of the playing schedule and points system that Sri Lanka qualified for the quarter-finals by dint of their opponents' forfeits.

Twelve countries, the largest ever and up from nine in 1992, took part in the competition. The new teams were United Arab Emirates, Netherlands and Kenya but the format of having two groups of six leading to the quarter-finals was later criticised. Sri Lanka had qualified effectively for reaching the knock-out stage before bowling a ball whilst England made it by beating only United Arab Emirates and Netherlands, the latter none too impressively. England did not beat any Test-playing nation as their proud World Cup record of previous competitions was dismantled. The format was shown up when unsurprisingly the most recent Test playing nation, Zimbabwe, and the Associate nations were eliminated as effectively only two victories were required to enter the knock-out stage.

With India hosting seventeen matches in seventeen venues, the travelling was made more arduous with some teams – as well as media with equipment – requiring sometimes two days to move between venues. Pakistan hosted sixteen matches over just six venues, Gujranwala being the only place with just one match. Sri Lanka had been allocated four games with three in Colombo and the other at the inland Kandy.

Another complaint was that this World Cup was too commercial, with sponsors paying vast amounts of money to acquire the status of the official sponsor. Coca-Cola and Pepsi were two examples of the official and unofficial companies involved. The tournament's official name was the Wills World Cup.

The grand opening ceremony in Calcutta's Eden Gardens hit snags as the laser show went wrong and a charge was made against Jagmohan Dalmiya, the chairman of Pilcom, the body organising the event, for wasting public money. A later, unsavoury event towards the end of the tournament would further blight the Eden Gardens's reputation.

More interesting and different tactics were used. Sri Lanka used Sanath Jayasuriya and wicket-keeper, Romesh Kaluwitharana, as aggressive opening batsmen in an attempt to make a far greater number of runs in the first fifteen overs. They were not always successful, but it made for fascinating viewing and Sri Lanka, continuing in this vein with other top-order batsmen, always had a healthy platform. Pinch hitters – lower-order batsmen promoted much higher – were used, sometimes with success.

The tournament started at Ahmedabad with England's campaign beginning poorly with an 11-run defeat to New Zealand. Nathan Astle's century and dropped catches by England led to England being unable to chase 240 and the start of a sorry tournament for the team which had always reached the semi-finals of previous tournaments.

At Rawalpindi, South Africa impressively reached 321 for two after rain washed out the first day with Gary Kirsten scoring South Africa's highest World Cup score to date of 188 not out. It was also then the highest score in the World Cup. The match was also remembered for the Emirati captain, Sultan Zarawani, the only UAE-born player, appearing in a floppy sun hat which presumably displeased tearaway fast bowler, Allan Donald, enough for him to bowl a bouncer which hit Zarawani and forced him to have a hospital check-up after his brief innings had been ended shortly afterwards. Arshad Laiq and Shaukat Dukanwala gallantly added 80 for the ninth wicket providing the only instance of a ninth-wicket pair more than doubling the total in a World Cup match.

Whilst New Zealand continued their fine start with an easy win over Netherlands at Baroda, the World Cup was graced by its eldest player in Dutch opener, Nolan Clarke, who made his bow at the age of 47 years and 240 days overtaking the previous incumbent, Zimbabwe's John Traicos, whose World Cup career ended at 44 years and 306 days.

Sri Lanka turned up for their first match at the R. Premadasa Stadium in Colombo but, when Australia did not, they were awarded the points. The same result was awarded eight days later against West Indies but, in between, the Zimbabweans were greeted warmly in Colombo although the hosts won comfortably.

England prevailed over United Arab Emirates at Peshawar easily whilst Zarawani continued to abstain from wearing a helmet. Neil Smith picked up the match award for three cheap wickets and 27 not out which ended retired hurt after a bout of sickness.

New Zealand, sporting a quicker attack whilst still maintaining the slower variety which had been so successful in 1992, were brought down to earth at Faisalabad where South Africa, who would impressively reach the quarter-finals without losing a match, beat them by five wickets.

India warmed up comfortably with wins over Kenya at Cuttack and West Indies at Gwalior. Australia, after finally beginning their campaign at Visakhapatnam against Kenya with a comfortable 97-run victory which included the World Cup's first-ever 200 partnership between Mark and Steve Waugh, then met India at Mumbai.

Mark Waugh became the first cricketer to score consecutive World Cup centuries but, after an opening century stand between him and captain Mark Taylor, five run outs rather spoiled proceedings and Australia had to settle for 258 after a late collapse. Tendulkar hit 90 in front of his home crowd but the loss of wickets regularly and especially to Damien Fleming meant that Australia emerged winners by 16 runs.

Slightly earlier, Zimbabwe and Kenya had to play each other twice at Patna after the first game was abandoned due to rain on the main, scheduled day. Zimbabwe, in some strife at 45 for three at the time of the abandonment, returned the next day to comfortably defeat their opponents through Paul Strang's five for 21, his side's best bowling figures in the World Cup and only occasion of a five-wicket haul for them.

After England's unconvincing victory over Netherlands (which included three players aged over 40) again at Peshawar, they were easily overcome by South Africa at Rawalpindi by 78 runs.

The shock of the tournament and one of the biggest upsets in the history of the World Cup happened at Pune when West Indies were dismissed well short of their modest victory target of 167 against Kenya. Indeed, they were dismissed for just 93 which was not only significantly their lowest, completed total in a World Cup match but was also the fourth occasion of an Associate nation defeating a Test playing one at the World Cup. It may have proved to be a watershed because, after a prior defeat to India, West Indies would pick up and become a threat in the competition.

Whilst South Africa blew aside all competition put in front of them (including another large total of 328 for three against Netherlands again at Rawalpindi) and Australia continuing in much the same way after their forfeit at Colombo, the battle of the Associate members, United Arab Emirates and Netherlands, at Lahore was won by the Middle Eastern side through Dukanwala's five for 29, still comfortably their best-ever bowling figures in two visits at the World Cup. A good batting display saw them successfully chase 217 for the loss of just three wickets.

The full extent of Sri Lanka's opening batsmen was felt by the Indian bowlers at Delhi when in response to India's 271 for three, Jayasuriya and Kaluwitharana made 42 from three overs mostly from Manoj Prabhakar who would play no further international cricket after this match. Tendulkar's 137 and an unbeaten 72 from captain Mohammad Azharuddin seemed to have set Sri Lanka a tough target but, despite a calmer period, Sri Lanka won by six wickets with eight balls remaining.

A necessary but impressive performance at Jaipur saw West Indies redeem themselves four days after their poor performance against Kenya and beat the hitherto undefeated and much-fancied Australians by six wickets. Captain Richie Richardson's unbeaten 93 ultimately outshone Ricky Ponting's maiden World Cup century.

After their victory against West Indies, Kenya came up against the Sri Lankan juggernaut in full flow at Kandy and conceded the then record ODI total of 398 for five which overtook England's 363 for seven against Pakistan in 1992. Aravinda de Silva's 145 was Sri Lanka's first-ever World Cup century and he would add to this eleven days later. Spiritedly as Kenya batted, they were easily overcome by 144 runs despite Steve Tikolo's 96.

With England being defeated by Pakistan in Karachi by the same result and almost identical scores as the 1987 encounter, they were pleased for their two victories over the Associates to take their place in the quarter-finals where the knock-out matches guaranteed the serious end of the World Cup.

In Faisalabad, England came up against the rampant Sri Lankan side where their first poor tournament performance since the World Cup's inception saw them defeated by five wickets with almost ten overs remaining. Philip de Freitas's elevation in the order saw him top score with 67 but England's 235 for eight (after being 173 for seven) was still unlikely to be sufficient especially after Jayasuriya's 44-ball 82 took Sri Lanka almost halfway to their target with almost three-quarters of their overs remaining.

India took on Pakistan at Bangalore and the match was Pakistan's first ODI against their opponents in India since October 1989. An impassioned match started with Wasim Akram ruled out through injury and a frenzied atmosphere saw India win the toss and score 287 for eight with Man of the Match Sidhu scoring 93. Ajay Jadeja bludgeoned 40 runs from Waqar Younis's final two overs. The left-handed opening combination of Aamer Sohail and Saeed Anwar started breathtakingly and gave the visitors a fine chance before both departed when well set. The adventurous start was negated by three wickets apiece by Kumble and Venkatesh Prasad leaving Pakistan 39 runs short of a semi-final spot and Javed Miandad's six-tournament World Cup career ended in disappointment.

A greater surprise took place in Karachi where the unbeaten South Africa lost by 19 runs to the improving West Indies. In a match where the spinners predominantly prevailed, Brian Lara's first World Cup century saw West Indies through to their first semi-final (and last to date) since 1983.

Australia had won both of their previous World Cup matches at Chennai (formerly Madras) but had their work cut out after New Zealand had won the toss and made an impressive 286 for nine. Chris

Harris's only ODI century, 130, coupled with wicket-keeper/captain Lee Germon's 89 gave New Zealand the chance to reach their fourth World Cup semi-final. It was not to be as Mark Waugh's third century of the competition saw the 1987 winners through with 2.1 overs remaining. New Zealand's total remains the highest losing first innings total in the World Cup from the quarter-final stages onwards.

Two vastly contrasting semi-finals took place between India and Sri Lanka at Calcutta and Australia and West Indies at Mohali. After the glitches experienced at the Eden Gardens opening ceremony, Sri Lanka reached their first-ever World Cup final after the match was called off after a section of the crowd caused a disturbance and set fire to some seats after India, having initially made a good start in pursuit of 252, subsided from 98 for one to 120 for eight.

The match had started promisingly for India after Jayasuriya and Kaluwitharana's belligerent shots had ended up in third man's hands in the first over. Aravinda de Silva's impressive tournament continued with 66 but he was fourth out at 85. Thanks to a fifty from Roshan Mahanama and scores of 30 from captain Ranatunga and Tillakaratne, Sri Lanka were able to post a reasonable total.

Once Tendulkar's 65 had been ended, the rest of the Indian batting collapsed and the disturbance in the crowd led to match referee Clive Lloyd bringing the teams off the field. A re-start was attempted but eventually the match was awarded to Sri Lanka in disappointing circumstances.

The heyday of West Indies seemed to be returning at Mohali as Australia faltered to 15 for four after opting to bat first. That they ultimately managed 207 for eight was due to a fifth-wicket partnership of 138 between Michael Bevan and Stuart Law but it seemed unlikely to be enough as West Indies reached 165 for two needing just 43 from the final nine overs.

Four wickets for Shane Warne upset the West Indian equilibrium and a remarkable collapse ensued and despite Richardson still being there as the last over started, it was Australia who prevailed by just five runs and entered their third final. Australia therefore finally met Sri Lanka but in Lahore.

Ranatunga broke with recent tradition by inserting Australia – the first three World Cup finals had all seen the toss-winning captain field first and ultimately lose but the toss (and match) had been won in 1987 and 1992 by the captain who batted first – and although initially it did not pay off due mainly to Mark Taylor's 74, Sri Lanka did apply the brakes through their spinners, de Silva's three for 42 being the best return in Australia's 241 for seven.

Kaluwitharana and Jayasuriya were dismissed early but their loss was quickly negated by Asanka Gurusinha, who finished a fine tournament with 65. With the dew making it difficult for the bowlers, Warne was comparatively expensive and the day belonged to de Silva who became the first player since Viv Richards in 1979 to record a century. From 23 for two, Sri Lanka cruised to an impressive seven-wicket victory in the first day/night game held in Pakistan. Having competed in all World Cups until their moment of glory, this was not only Sri Lanka's finest hour but also the first time in which they had reached the knock-out stage.

1996 MISCELLANY

- The Dutch side against England at Peshawar had the oldest average age of any World Cup team at 33 years and 293 days.
- Javed Miandad ended his six tournament World Cup after a so far unsurpassed span of 20 years and 273 days.
- Dutch wicket-keeper, Marcel Schewe, did not concede a bye during the competition. Whilst other wicket-keepers have achieved the same, Schewe's five-match career is to date the most by a player in a complete World Cup career. Schewe claimed three victims in the first match but none thereafter.
- The West Indies and Kenya match saw the only time in the World Cup – but third time in all ODIs – that extras was the top-scorer in the match.
- Sri Lanka became the first team in six World Cup finals to win batting second.
- Mark Waugh became the first player to score three centuries in a World Cup competition.
- Pakistan's Ramiz Raja holds the record for most World Cup runs (700) without hitting a six. His 16-match career ended during the 1996 tournament.

1996 STATISTICS

HIGHEST TOTALS	
398 for 5 in 50 overs	Sri Lanka vs. Kenya at Kandy
328 for 3 in 50 overs	South Africa vs. Netherlands at Rawalpindi
321 for 2 in 50 overs	South Africa vs. United Arab Emirates at Rawalpindi
307 for 8 in 50 overs	New Zealand vs. Netherlands at Baroda
304 for 7 in 50 overs	Australia vs. Kenya at Visakhapatnam

LOWEST COMPLETED TOTALS	
93 in 35.2 overs	West Indies vs. Kenya at Pune
109 for 9 in 33 overs	United Arab Emirates vs. Pakistan at Gujranwala
120 for 8 in 34.1 overs	India vs. Sri Lanka at Calcutta
134 in 49.4 overs	Kenya vs. Zimbabwe at Patna
136 in 48.3 overs	United Arab Emirates vs. England at Peshawar

HIGHEST MATCH AGGREGATES	
652 for 12 wickets	Sri Lanka (398-5) vs. Kenya (254-7) at Kandy
575 for 13 wickets	New Zealand (286-9) vs. Australia (289-4) at Chennai
543 for 7 wickets	India (271-3) vs. Sri Lanka (272-4) at Delhi

LOWEST MATCH AGGREGATES WITH RESULT	
221 for 10 wickets	United Arab Emirates (109-9) vs. Pakistan (112-1) at Gujranwala
259 for 20 wickets	Kenya (166) vs. West Indies (93) at Pune
271 for 15 wickets	Kenya (134) vs. Zimbabwe (137-5) at Patna
276 for 12 wickets	United Arab Emirates (136) vs. England (140-2) at Peshawar

BIGGEST VICTORY MARGINS	
169 runs	South Africa (321-2) vs. United Arab Emirates (152-8) at Rawalpindi
160 runs	South Africa (328-3) vs. Netherlands (168-8) at Rawalpindi
144 runs	Sri Lanka (398-5) vs. Kenya (254-7) at Kandy
9 wickets	Pakistan (112-1) vs. United Arab Emirates (109-9) at Gujranwala

LOWEST VICTORY MARGINS	
5 runs	Australia (207-8) vs. West Indies (202) at Mohali
11 runs	New Zealand (239-6) vs. England (228-9) at Ahmedabad
4 wickets	West Indies (232-6) vs. Australia (229-6) at Jaipur

LEADING RUN SCORERS	
523 (average 87.17)	Sachin Tendulkar (India)
484 (average 80.67)	Mark Waugh (Australia)
448 (average 89.60)	Aravinda de Silva (Sri Lanka)

HIGHEST SCORES		
188*	Gary Kirsten	South Africa vs. United Arab Emirates at Rawalpindi
161	Andrew Hudson	South Africa vs. Netherlands at Rawalpindi
145	Aravinda de Silva	Sri Lanka vs. Kenya at Kandy
137	Sachin Tendulkar	India vs. Sri Lanka at Delhi
130	Mark Waugh	Australia vs. Kenya at Visakhapatnam
130	Chris Harris	New Zealand vs. Australia at Chennai

CENTURIES
Sixteen

LEADING WICKET TAKERS	
15 (average 18.73)	Anil Kumble (India)
13 (average 19.46)	Waqar Younis (Pakistan)

BEST BOWLING PERFORMANCES		
9.4-1-21-5	Paul Strang	Zimbabwe vs. Kenya at Patna
10-0-29-5	Shaukat Dukanwala	United Arab Emirates vs. Netherlands at Lahore
9-0-36-5	Damien Fleming	Australia vs. India at Mumbai

FIVE WICKETS IN AN INNINGS
Three

HIGHEST PARTNERSHIPS FOR EACH WICKET				
1	186	Gary Kirsten & Andrew Hudson	SA vs. Neth	Rawalpindi
2	138	Shivnarine Chanderpaul & Brian Lara	WI vs. SA	Karachi
3	207	Mark Waugh & Steve Waugh	Aus. vs. Ken	Visakhapatnam
4	168	Lee Germon & Chris Harris	NZ vs. Aus	Chennai
5	138	Stuart Law & Michael Bevan	Aus. vs. WI	Mohali
6	80*	Salim Malik & Wasim Akram	Pak. vs. NZ	Lahore
7	44	Hitesh Modi & Thomas Odoyo	Ken. vs. WI	Pune
8	62	Dermot Reeve & Darren Gough	Eng. vs. SL	Faisalabad
9	80*	Arshad Laiq & Shaukat Dukanwala	UAE vs. SA	Rawalpindi
10	17	Chris Matthews & Fanie de Villiers	SA vs. Eng.	Rawalpindi
	17	Chris Matthews & Paul Adams	SA vs. WI	Karachi

1999

After sixteen years, the World Cup returned to England for the fourth time. The first two tournaments had seen just thirty matches between them and although 1983 had included twenty-seven, there had been only fifty-seven matches between all three. 1999 had forty-two, the most of any World Cup at that stage.

It also included a new format. Rather than teams playing each other either entirely in a round-robin or group stage, a new concept of a Super Six stage was introduced. It meant that the two initial groups of six were whittled down to three from each group after playing each other and the six remaining teams went into the new Super Six stage. Those who qualified carried forward their points from the group stage against the other two qualifiers from their original group into the Super Six. Each side then played the qualifiers from the other group from where one further team from each pool would be eliminated leaving the four remaining sides to contest the semi-finals. In the earlier stages, a now more familiar net run rate rule – but not so obvious then – could also be used for progression to the latter stages should there be a tie on points at the end of the group stage.

Matches were held predominantly in England, Wales, Scotland and Ireland but one surprise was that South Africa and Kenya were despatched to Holland to play at Amstelveen just outside Amsterdam. This ground would later host further, more regular, ODIs five years later.

Twelve teams again featured with Bangladesh and Scotland being welcomed for the first time having qualified via the 1997 ICC Trophy. These teams came in at the expense of United Arab Emirates and Netherlands.

The tournament started in the middle of May with a lacklustre opening ceremony which saw a few fireworks and balloons released on a dull, drizzly day at Lord's. The curtain-raiser saw the main hosts pitted against defending champions Sri Lanka at Lord's. It proved to be a one-sided spectacle with England romping home by eight wickets after requiring just 205 to win. Sri Lanka's was a disappointing defence of their title as they were eliminated before the Super Six stage. England, though, won three of their first four games but their at times slightly pedestrian approach to victory and a poor batting performance against South Africa made a potential advance to the Super Six stage trickier than it might have been.

Some creative thinking in another early game was seized upon and ended by the first drinks break. South African coach, Bob Woolmer, had given advice to captain Hansie Cronje and Allan Donald by means of a one-way radio system in the South Africa and India game at Hove and the practice was quickly banned. South Africa prevailed without further radio help and the all-round talents which would have such a profound impression on the tournament of Lance Klusener were quickly visible.

Scotland and Bangladesh both lost their first World Cup games although Scotland performed creditably against Australia. Kenya would have little to show for their efforts and were unable to spring a further surprise on their opponents despite Steve Tikolo's two fifties during their five matches.

Sachin Tendulkar had to return to India after the death of his father but most creditably soon returned after missing just the Zimbabwe game at Leicester. This bizarre match featured 90 extras and India being docked four overs for a very tardy over rate. Ultimately, after Zimbabwe's 252 for nine, India still seemed favourites until a returning Henry Olonga, after an erratic earlier spell, took three wickets in one over to give his side a three-run victory.

After Tendulkar's return, India finally notched up their first win with an easy victory over Kenya at Bristol after Tendulkar's imperious unbeaten 140 and Rahul Dravid's unbeaten 104 saw their side to 329 for two in a record third-wicket partnership of 237.

With Klusener in prime form for South Africa, English crowds were also treated to and at times quietened by the searing pace of Pakistan's Shoaib Akhtar. Despite Pakistan's top-order's fragility in the games against West Indies at Bristol and against Scotland at Chester-le-Street, they managed to prevail through batting recoveries and an impressive bowling line-up.

Australia continued their sluggish start with a five-wicket defeat against New Zealand at Cardiff, but England impressed with an easy victory over Kenya at Canterbury's first ODI. A subsequent heavy defeat to South Africa at The Oval, where they could only manage 103 in pursuit of a modest 226, seemed to give little cause for alarm after they defeated Zimbabwe at Trent Bridge. This game was again noticeable for England's overly cautious approach to their target of just 168 and for the elevation in the Zimbabwean batting order of Paul Strang as a pinch hitter which saw him finish with a 17-ball duck.

India's renaissance continued at Taunton with a resounding victory over Sri Lanka, due mainly to the still highest partnership in the World Cup in England of 318 between centurions Sourav Ganguly and Dravid.

Chelmsford sprung a surprise with Zimbabwe gaining a 48-run victory over South Africa. This match would have repercussions for both the vanquished side and the hosts, England. It also took Zimbabwe through to the Super Six stage.

Australia lost to Pakistan by just ten runs in a fine game at Headingley but were back on track chasing down a victory target of 179 against Bangladesh at Chester-le-Street in just 19.5 overs.

There was a shock in the same group when Bangladesh surprisingly overcame Pakistan at Northampton by 62 runs which led to mutterings of malpractice. Australia overcame West Indies in a turgid match at Old Trafford where the victors saw themselves through to the Super Six stage exploiting a gremlin in the tournament rules which may not have been apparent at the start of the tournament to ensure their progress to the next round.

Due to South Africa's defeat to Zimbabwe, England's game against India at Edgbaston suddenly became a must-win for the hosts. Rain made for an anxious wait after play ended on the first day with England at 73 for three chasing 233. When play resumed, they did not come close, losing by 63 runs and were knocked out for the first time at the group stage.

Pakistan, Zimbabwe, South Africa, New Zealand, India and Australia therefore qualified for the Super Six stage from which two further teams would be eliminated. There would be some fine games during this second stage before the semi-finals.

Australia overcame India at The Oval after an inspired early burst from McGrath had put India on the back foot in pursuit of 283. An Ajay Jadeja century and 75 from Robin Singh failed to save the 1983 winners.

A topsy-turvy match at Trent Bridge saw South Africa seal an unlikely victory over Pakistan. A modest score of 220 for seven seemed likely to be enough as South Africa stumbled to 58 for five. Captain Cronje had promoted himself but been caught at third man from another Akhtar thunderbolt. The recovery was initiated through Jacques Kallis and Shaun Pollock before Klusener bludgeoned an unbeaten 46 to guide South Africa home by three wickets with one over remaining.

Poor weather saw the only no result of the tournament between New Zealand and Zimbabwe whilst India maintained their World Cup stranglehold over neighbours Pakistan with a 47-run win at Old Trafford. Security was very tight due to a conflict between both countries' armies over Kashmir.

A Neil Johnson century against Australia at Lord's raised the possibility that Zimbabwe might repeat their famous 1983 victory despite a target of 304 being set. Ultimately, their challenge fizzled out but Johnson, who would regularly open the batting and bowling, proved himself a worthy all-rounder.

South Africa saw off New Zealand at Edgbaston whilst Pakistan impressively defeated Zimbabwe by 148 runs at The Oval to secure their third semi-final in England. Their entrance was confirmed through Saqlain Mushtaq's hat-trick, only the second in the World Cup and almost twelve years after Chetan Sharma's. New Zealand rallied to also reach the semi-finals with a five-wicket victory over India at Trent Bridge. This was their third semi-final appearance in England and fourth in total.

A dramatic match at Headingley saw Australia qualify for the semi-finals with a five-wicket victory with just two balls remaining over South Africa, who they would then meet in the knock-out stage. Herschelle Gibbs's second ODI hundred in 35 innings set Australia a testing target of 272 which seemed that much larger when the first three wickets fell for just 48. It was, though, Gibbs's dropping of Steve Waugh after possibly appearing to celebrate the routine catch prematurely which allowed Australia back in. Waugh, needing no further encouragement, upstaged his dropper's earlier 101 by finishing with a vital unbeaten

120. If it was possible to repeat such an exhilarating match, the same sides would do so just four days later.

The first semi-final at Old Trafford saw an impressive bowling and batting performance by Pakistan which consigned New Zealand for the fourth time to the role of bridesmaids and being knocked out before the final. A trio of 40s and the top score of 47 coming from Extras saw New Zealand to 241 for seven but it was always too small a target once Saeed Anwar, blossoming towards the end of the tournament with consecutive hundreds, and Wajahatullah Wasti added 194 for the first wicket. Pakistan entered their second final with a nine-wicket victory. Geoff Allott's impressive performance of 20 wickets in the tournament, at that stage the most by any bowler in the World Cup, went unrewarded by a final appearance.

The second semi-final laid claim to being the most memorable in World Cup and even ODI history. The Edgbaston crowd saw a match of 426 runs and 20 wickets and, at its dramatic denouement, the sides could not be separated. A poor Australian start was repaired again by captain Waugh and Michael Bevan but four ducks and five wickets for Shaun Pollock and four from Allan Donald left South Africa needing 214.

They had a fine start before Shane Warne's best form came to the fore and 48 for none became 61 for four. A partnership of 84 between Jacques Kallis and Jonty Rhodes seemed to be taking South Africa to the winning line but Warne's dismissal of Kallis again left the match evenly balanced. With wickets continuing to fall, South Africa's final pair of Man of the Tournament Klusener and Donald needed to find 16 runs and Klusener's latest pummelling equalled the scores with four balls remaining. Donald was almost run out from the next ball and a mix-up the following ball ensured that the non-striking Donald was indeed run out after a relay amongst the fielders and the ball being rolled up the pitch. Australia reached the final by virtue of their higher position in the final Super Six table (achieved by a superior net run rate).

If the second semi-final was one of the closest and most memorable ODIs played, the final was not. Pakistan decided to bat but, like their semi-final against New Zealand, Extras was the highest scorer. In the semi-final, Pakistan had been the culprits in making this

New Zealand's highest score, but the reverse was the case in the final, Australia conceding 25 as Pakistan subsided for just 132. It is still the lowest score in a final and Warne added four further wickets to the four he took in the semi-final.

Australia's simple victory was achieved from the first ball of the twenty-first over, Mark Waugh finishing unbeaten on 37 after Adam Gilchrist's opening salvo of 54 had helped realise 75 for the first wicket. The match lasted just 59.1 overs and took just over four-and-a-half hours of playing time as Australia romped to their second World Cup victory. The twentieth century ended with this Australian victory and they would single-handedly monopolise the first decade of the twenty-first, not losing a further match until 2011.

1999 MISCELLANY

- Neil Johnson opened both the batting and bowling in a match six times for Zimbabwe, the most by any player in the World Cup. No-one else has performed the same feat more than three times.
- Thirteen of the top twenty occasions of most extras in an innings occurred in the 1999 tournament.
- The aggregate of 265 runs is the lowest of any World Cup final. The 1983 final is second-lowest with 323 runs.
- West Indian wicket-keeper Ridley Jacobs is the only batsman to carry his bat through a completed World Cup innings (in which the team batting has been dismissed).
- The Indian innings against Australia at The Oval saw the only occasion in a completed ODI innings of one batsman scoring a century, one other fifty and all other batsmen dismissed without reaching double figures.

1999 STATISTICS

HIGHEST TOTALS	
373 for 6 in 50 overs	India vs. Sri Lanka at Taunton
329 for 2 in 50 overs	India vs. Kenya at Bristol
303 for 4 in 50 overs	Australia vs. Zimbabwe at Lord's

LOWEST COMPLETED TOTALS

68 in 31.3 overs	Scotland vs. West Indies at Leicester
103 in 41 overs	England vs. South Africa at The Oval
110 in 46.4 overs	West Indies vs. Australia at Manchester
110 in 35.2 overs	Sri Lanka vs. South Africa at Northampton

HIGHEST MATCH AGGREGATES

589 for 16 wickets	India (373-6) vs. Sri Lanka (216) at Taunton
564 for 9 wickets	India (329-2) vs. Kenya (235-7) at Bristol
562 for 10 wickets	Australia (303-4) vs. Zimbabwe (259-6) at Lord's

LOWEST MATCH AGGREGATES WITH RESULT

138 for 12 wickets	Scotland (68) vs. West Indies (70-2) at Leicester
221 for 14 wickets	West Indies (110) vs. Australia (111-4) at Manchester
233 for 14 wickets	Bangladesh (116) vs. New Zealand (117-4) at Chelmsford
244 for 14 wickets	Scotland (121) vs. New Zealand (123-4) at Edinburgh

BIGGEST VICTORY MARGINS

157 runs	India (373-6) vs. Sri Lanka (216) at Taunton
148 runs	Pakistan (271-9) vs. Zimbabwe (123) at The Oval
9 wickets	England (204-1) vs. Kenya (203) at Canterbury
9 wickets	Pakistan (242-1) vs. New Zealand (241-7) at Manchester

LOWEST VICTORY MARGINS

Tied match	Australia (213) vs. South Africa (213) at Birmingham * (Australia won by superior position in Super Six table)
3 runs	Zimbabwe (252-9) vs. India (249) at Leicester
10 runs	Pakistan (275-8) vs. Australia (265) at Leeds
3 wickets	South Africa (221-7) vs. Pakistan (220-7) at Nottingham

LEADING RUN SCORERS

461 (average 65.86)	Rahul Dravid (India)
398 (average 79.60)	Steve Waugh (Australia)
379 (average 54.14)	Sourav Ganguly (India)
375 (average 41.67)	Mark Waugh (Australia)

HIGHEST SCORES

183	Sourav Ganguly	India vs. Sri Lanka at Taunton
145	Rahul Dravid	India vs. Sri Lanka at Taunton
140*	Sachin Tendulkar	India vs. Kenya at Bristol
132*	Neil Johnson	Zimbabwe vs. Australia at Lord's
120*	Steve Waugh	Australia vs. South Africa at Leeds

CENTURIES

Eleven

LEADING WICKET SCORERS

20 (average 16.25)	Geoff Allott (New Zealand)
20 (average 18.05)	Shane Warne (Australia)
18 (average 20.39)	Glenn McGrath (Australia)

BEST BOWLING PERFORMANCES

8.4-3-14-5	Glenn McGrath	Australia vs. West Indies at Manchester
8.3-3-21-5	Lance Klusener	South Africa vs. Kenya at Amsterdam
9.3-2-27-5	Venkatesh Prasad	India vs. Pakistan at Manchester
9.3-0-31-5	Robin Singh	India vs. Sri Lanka at Taunton
10-1-35-5	Saqlain Mushtaq	Pakistan vs. Bangladesh at Northampton
9.2-1-36-5	Shaun Pollock	South Africa vs. Australia at Birmingham

FIVE WICKETS IN AN INNINGS

Six

HIGHEST PARTNERSHIPS FOR EACH WICKET

1	194	Saeed Anwar & Wajahatullah Wasti	Pak. vs. NZ	Manchester
2	318	Sourav Ganguly & Rahul Dravid	Ind. vs. SL	Taunton
3	237*	Rahul Dravid & Sachin Tendulkar	Ind. vs. Ken.	Bristol
4	126	Ricky Ponting & Steve Waugh	Aus. vs. SA	Leeds
5	148	Roger Twose & Chris Cairns	NZ vs. Aus.	Cardiff
6	161	Maurice Odumbe & Alpesh Vadher	Ken. vs. SL	Southampton
7	83	Stephen Fleming & Chris Harris	NZ vs. Pak	Derby
8	64	Mahela Jayawardene & Chaminda Vaas	SL vs. Ken.	Southampton
9	44	Lance Klusener & Steve Elworthy	SA vs. SL	Northampton
10	35	Lance Klusener & Allan Donald	SA vs. Zim	Chelmsford

2003

In 2003, the World Cup was held for the first time in predominantly South Africa with Kenya and Zimbabwe also hosting games. All three African teams were part of the 14-team set up with Namibia also included.

The 2003 event remains the biggest tournament to date with no other World Cup before or since matching the fifty-four matches held. With fourteen teams being also the largest number ever to participate and forty-three days were required to complete the epic tournament. Two pools of seven teams required forty-two matches and twenty-four days to complete before the field was whittled down to six sides contesting another Super Six stage. Points would again be carried forward for wins over fellow Super Six qualifiers and reduced points for wins over teams eliminated before this stage.

Pool A saw Australia, England, Netherlands, India, Namibia, Pakistan and Zimbabwe contest the group whilst Pool B included Bangladesh, Canada (making their first appearance since 1979), Kenya, New Zealand, South Africa, Sri Lanka and West Indies.

Much action on the field was promised during the marathon tournament and there was much off it also. On the verge of the tournament, Australia found themselves without Shane Warne who was banned for taking a diuretic which included a banned substance. If, though, his absence might have been sorely felt, others stood up with impressive performances and other than a couple of close games on a slow Port Elizabeth pitch, they were rarely greatly inconvenienced.

Like the 1996 event, some teams were anxious about security issues in Nairobi and Harare. New Zealand would decline to play in Nairobi and England in Harare, the latter after receiving threats from a group called Sons and Daughters of Zimbabwe. The New Zealand experience of pulling out of their match against Kenya was simpler with their board making the decision. England's players found themselves in an invidious and much-publicised position and their eventual withdrawal meant that, like New Zealand, the points were given to their opponents. The impact of not playing would boost the chances of both the home teams.

India were also a doubt with their participation after a dispute over product endorsement although ultimately they did take part.

South Africa's strong performances in World Cups since their readmission to international cricket made them a potentially strong foe for any opponent. Twice semi-finalists and on the other occasion reaching the quarter-finals, it would become a blow on the first day of the 2003 tournament when a Brian Lara century helped the West Indies inflict a three-run defeat on the hosts. It was their second defeat in as many games to the West Indies in the World Cup, the previous one in 1996 putting them out of that year's tournament.

The second day of the tournament was even more dramatic in the Pool A game between Zimbabwe and Namibia at Harare. Zimbabwean players Andy Flower and Henry Olonga wore black armbands after issuing a statement mourning 'the death of democracy in our beloved Zimbabwe' after human rights issues by Robert Mugabe's regime. Olonga would play just one further ODI for Zimbabwe after this in Bloemfontein after a no result against Pakistan secured Zimbabwe's participation in the Super Six and with no games being held in Zimbabwe during this second stage, a flight to freedom for Olonga. Flower's impressive international career would also end with Zimbabwe's exit in the competition.

Craig Wishart's unbeaten 172 in this game, the highest score of the competition, helped Zimbabwe to a simple Duckworth-Lewis win although there had been a chance that the match could have ended very slightly earlier, which would have dashed their victory hopes.

1992 winners and 1999 finalists, Pakistan, endured a poor tournament and the no result in the last pool game against Zimbabwe sent Zimbabwe to South Africa and Pakistan home. Their two wins came only against Namibia and Netherlands. Wasim Akram celebrated his 500th ODI wicket and Shoaib Akhtar bowled the first officially-recorded 100 mph delivery but it could not take away a disappointing team performance.

England, despite their off-field distractions, played far better cricket than they had in 1996 and 1999 but their withdrawal from the Harare game ultimately cost them a better chance of a place in the Super Six. An easy win over the Netherlands at East London was followed by victory over Namibia at Port Elizabeth although there was a time when Namibia, through Jan-Berrie Burger, one of three Namibian players with the same surname, threatened an upset with 85 in 86 balls. Former Namibian rugby player, Rudi van Vuuren, had earlier taken five wickets but England, despite Namibia being ahead on Duckworth-Lewis, survived.

James Anderson started to make his name with four Pakistani wickets at Cape Town and a more impressive victory was only denied by Shoaib Akhtar's 43 which remains the highest score in the World Cup by a number 11.

A poor batting performance against India (in which Ashish Nehra's six for 23 was and still remains India's best World Cup performance) at Durban left England facing Australia in their final pool game at Port Elizabeth. It proved to be a cracker of a match and one which England probably expected to win after reducing Australia to 135 for eight in pursuit of a modest 205. That they did not was due to an astonishing all-round performance from Australia's Andy Bichel who firstly dismantled England with seven for 20 and then calmly, with the support of one of cricket's greatest finishers, Michael Bevan, saw his side home without further loss with just two balls left. It would prove enough to send England home and for Australia to retain their unbeaten record in the tournament to date.

Until that point, Australia's all-conquering march had actually started shakily against Pakistan at Wanderers with four wickets falling for 86. Andrew Symonds's undefeated 143 – his maiden ODI century in his 55th match – saw the early damage repaired and lead his side to a 82-run win. A demolition of India at Centurion Park was followed by victories over the Netherlands and Zimbabwe before their fifth pool match saw them take on Namibia at Potchefstroom.

Three individual fifties from Hayden, Symonds and Lehmann took Australia to 301 for six before Glenn McGrath reduced Namibia to just 45 all out. McGrath's seven for 15 remains the World Cup's best bowling figures.

India's campaign started with a wobble against Holland at Paarl after being dismissed for only 204. Ultimately, it proved ample but a further poor batting display against Australia (managing only 125) left them vulnerable. They came back very strongly with eight consecutive wins. They atoned for their three-run loss to Zimbabwe in the 1999 tournament by beating the same opponents by 83 runs at Harare whilst centuries from Tendulkar and captain Ganguly against Namibia helped complete a 181-run victory. Nehra's six-wicket burst against England left their last pool game against their neighbours, Pakistan, at Centurion.

It proved to be one of the most exciting matches of the tournament with Saeed Anwar's 101 taking Pakistan to 273 for seven. Tendulkar's 98 included an opening, breathtaking blitz on Shoaib Akhtar and again it was India who prevailed once again by six wickets with over four overs in hand.

Netherlands showed promise although their only win was against Namibia. Feiko Kloppenburg and Klaas-Jan van Noortwijk both made centuries and Kloppenburg added four wickets in the Namibian innings for one of the most impressive all-round World Cup performances.

Although Namibia regularly conceded 300 runs, their performance in bowling out England and batting spiritedly was remembered and they took nine Pakistani wickets in conceding only 255 runs.

In Pool B, Lance Klusener carried his 1999 form into the 2003 tournament. He narrowly missed out on taking his side home against West Indies but four wickets at Potchefstroom against Kenya ensured an easy ten-wicket victory. Despite scoring 306 against New Zealand at Wanderers, a career-best, undefeated 134 by Stephen Fleming saw New Zealand easily achieve a reduced target in a vital match for both sides. As it happened, it was South Africa facing elimination before the Super Six stage after this defeat to New Zealand.

South Africa secured another ten-wicket victory over Bangladesh at Bloemfontein and a 118-run win over Canada at East London but their last pool match against Sri Lanka at Durban proved to be their undoing. Needing a win, the rain came with the hosts on 229 for six thinking that they had done just enough to win the match and progress to the Super Six. A misreading of the Duckworth-Lewis score, though, meant that the match was tied and this latest tie ensured that their interest in the tournament ended.

Meanwhile, New Zealand won four of their games despite not travelling to Nairobi and would make the Super Six stage with third place in the group.

After a heavy defeat to South Africa in their first game, Kenya played fine cricket to record successive victories over Canada and two Test playing nations, Sri Lanka and Bangladesh. In their captain, Steve Tikolo, they had a fine all-rounder who performed admirably throughout the tournament. Another experienced all-rounder, Maurice Odumbe, also enjoyed his moments with bat and ball but one of the finds of the tournament was Collins Obuya who captured thirteen wickets in the tournament including five against Sri Lanka at Nairobi, Kenya's only five-wicket haul in their World Cup history. Obuya's brother, Kennedy Otieno, also performed creditably with the bat.

Whilst New Zealand's forfeit in Nairobi undoubtedly helped Kenya's chances, they deserved their position in the Super Six and were the surprise of the tournament.

Canada was another team who returned home with only one victory but there were some memorable and rousing performances especially from their star all-rounder, John Davison. Their win came in their very first match against Bangladesh when they comfortably defended 180, tearaway fast bowler Austin Codrington taking five for 27, Canada's best bowling figures.

Whilst picking up useful wickets with his off breaks, Davison served notice of his talents with a withering assault on a presumably bemused West Indian attack including Merv Dillon, Pedro Collins and Vasbert Drakes and made 111 in only 76 balls, his hundred coming in a then record 67 balls. The match may not have ended with a happy result for Canada, but Davison's talents were the talk of the tournament.

Alas, before the West Indian match, Canada were the beaten team in the World Cup's shortest match. Paarl witnessed just 23 overs as Canada, put in to bat, were dismissed for 36 and Sri Lanka won with 272 balls remaining. Canada's total is still the World Cup's lowest completed total.

Sri Lanka headed Pool B with impressive victories over New Zealand and Bangladesh. The latter match at Pietermaritzburg started in bizarre fashion with Chaminda Vaas taking a hat-trick with the first three balls of the match and adding another wicket before the over was out with Bangladesh a somewhat parlous five for four.

After dismantling Canada, they came unstuck in Nairobi against worthy winners Kenya. Their 53-run defeat may have been a surprise, but it was also a complete reversal of their 1996 encounter when Sri Lanka made 398 for five which was still the highest ODI total at the time of their re-match in 2003. They would have a narrow win over West Indies at Cape Town before the exciting tie at Durban against South Africa.

Bangladesh endured a forlorn tournament losing to non-Test playing countries Canada and Kenya and suffering two ten-wicket defeats to Sri Lanka and South Africa. They lost all their games bar the match at Benoni against West Indies which was abandoned due to rain.

West Indies' stirring win in their first game did not, however, lead to a place in the Super Six. The abandonment at Benoni dampened their chances and, needing a victory against Sri Lanka at Cape Town, they fell just six runs short. Ramnaresh Sarwan, returning to the crease from hospital after being hit by a bouncer earlier in his innings, could not quite see his side through.

Australia, Kenya, India, Sri Lanka, New Zealand and Zimbabwe therefore qualified in that order for the Super Six stage with 8.5 points separating the top and bottom sides from the starting table.

After a century for Ricky Ponting and 99 from Adam Gilchrist, Australia ran out easy winners over Sri Lanka at Centurion. Brett Lee, who took twenty-two wickets in the competition and was one of the major forces, added to his existing tally with three wickets.

India overcame Kenya at Cape Town despite a poor start to their innings whilst New Zealand saw off Zimbabwe at Bloemfontein. Sachin Tendulkar's 673 runs in the tournament remains the most in any World Cup and, after a rare failure against Kenya, was back to his best with 97 against Sri Lanka at Johannesburg as India enjoyed a 183-run victory.

One of the games of this stage and indeed tournament was between Australia and New Zealand at Port Elizabeth. Fast bowler Shane Bond ripped through the Australian order to finish with six for 23 and at one stage had reduced the defending champions to 84 for seven. Bevan and Bichel again held sway and fashioned a recovery to 208 and with five wickets for Lee, New Zealand were dismissed well short at 112 all out.

At Bloemfontein, Kenya dismissed Zimbabwe for just 133 and, in reaching their target for the loss of just three wickets, qualified for the semi-finals. Theirs had been a remarkable performance and they are still the only non-Test playing country to reach the semi-finals of the World Cup.

Sri Lanka also qualified for the semi-finals with an eleventh hour victory over Zimbabwe. They therefore joined Australia, India and Kenya and the last remaining match of the Super Six stage was played between Australia and Kenya at Durban.

There was a surprise in store. Ultimately, Australia came through comfortably enough, but the match was remembered more for a spell of bowling than Brett Lee's earlier hat-trick. Aasif Karim, who also played Davis Cup tennis for Kenya, produced startling figures of 8.2-6-7-3 dismissing Ponting, Lehmann and Brad Hogg and his figures were slightly dented after being hit for the winning boundary.

Rain affected the Australia and Sri Lanka semi-final, but the match was made memorable for Gilchrist walking after knowing he had hit the ball despite being given not out. Despite their struggles on the Port Elizabeth pitch throughout the competition, Australia still managed to make 212 through Symonds's unbeaten 91 and it proved ample when the rain came, Australia being 48 runs ahead on Duckworth-Lewis.

There would be no repeat of the stutter by India in their Super Six game against Kenya and, at Durban, they ended Kenya's hopes. Tendulkar's 83 and Ganguly's second successive century against Kenya (and third in the tournament) saw India comfortably reach the final with a 91-run win.

India went into the Wanderers final against Australia having won their previous eight matches starting after their heavy defeat to their final opponents. The run ended against the same opponents. Sourav Ganguly decided to insert Australia and the plan did not pay off with Australia reaching a daunting 359 for two with big contributions from the few batsmen required. Captain Ponting with an undefeated 140 led the charge and became the first captain since Clive Lloyd in 1975 to score a century in a World Cup final. Australia's total is the highest in any final to date.

A good start was imperative for India facing such an intimidating total, but they did not receive it with Man of the Tournament Tendulkar being dismissed in the first over. Despite an aggressive 82 from Virender Sehwag and a more sedate 47 from Dravid, Australia retained their trophy with a 125-run victory, the largest in terms of runs in World Cup history.

2003 MISCELLANY

- 2003 is the only occasion of the tournament's highest total coming in the final.
- The runs aggregate of 593 for 12 wickets is the most of all 11 World Cup finals.
- Five of the top eight World Cup bowling performances came in 2003.
- The partnership of 42 between Namibia's Bjorn Kotze and Rudi van Vuuren is the only World Cup instance of a tenth-wicket pair doubling the total.
- Seven years after dismissing West Indies for just 93 at Pune, Kenya were dismissed for only 104 by the same opponents at Kimberley.
- Kenya's Aasif Karim became the first player since Mike Hendrick in 1979 to bowl six maidens in a World Cup innings. There have been twenty instances of bowlers bowling five or more but no-one has bowled six since Karim.
- Canada's 202 all out against West Indies at Centurion is the lowest completed World Cup total to include a century.
- Canada's 36 all out is the only instance in the World Cup of no batsman reaching double figures.
- Darren Lehmann's undefeated 50 in Australia's match against Namibia is the lowest individual ODI score to be more than the opposition's total.
- Port Elizabeth and Kimberley featured prominently with individual five wickets in an innings performances, Port Elizabeth achieving four (the second most at any World Cup ground behind Leeds) in five games and Kimberley with two in three matches.
- Chaminda Vaas's 23 wickets in the tournament is a World Cup record by a left-arm bowler.

2003 STATISTICS

HIGHEST TOTALS	
359 for 2 in 50 overs	Australia vs. India at Johannesburg
340 for 2 in 50 overs	Zimbabwe vs. Namibia at Harare
319 for 5 in 50 overs	Australia vs. Sri Lanka at Centurion
314 for 4 in 50 overs	Netherlands vs. Namibia at Bloemfontein
311 for 2 in 50 overs	India vs. Namibia at Pietermaritzburg

LOWEST COMPLETED TOTALS	
36 in 18.4 overs	Canada vs. Sri Lanka at Paarl
45 in 14 overs	Namibia vs. Australia at Potchefstroom
84 in 17.4 overs	Namibia vs. Pakistan at Kimberley
104 in 35.5 overs	Kenya vs. West Indies at Kimberley
108 in 35.1 overs	Bangladesh vs. South Africa at Bloemfontein

HIGHEST MATCH AGGREGATES	
593 for 12 wickets	Australia (359-2) vs. India (234) at Johannesburg
564 for 14 wickets	Netherlands (314-4) vs. Namibia (250) at Bloemfontein
553 for 14 wickets	West Indies (278-5) vs. South Africa (275-9) at Cape Town
549 for 11 wickets	Pakistan (273-7) vs. India (276-4) at Centurion

LOWEST MATCH AGGREGATES WITH RESULT	
73 for 11 wickets	Canada (36) vs. Sri Lanka (37-1) at Paarl
217 for 10 wickets	Bangladesh (108) vs. South Africa (109-0) at Bloemfontein
250 for 10 wickets	Bangladesh (124) vs. Sri Lanka (126-0) at Pietermaritzburg

BIGGEST VICTORY MARGINS	
256 runs	Australia (301-6) vs. Namibia (45) at Potchefstroom
183 runs	India (292-6) vs. Sri Lanka (109) at Johannesburg
181 runs	India (311-2) vs. Namibia (130) at Pietermaritzburg
171 runs	Pakistan (255-9) vs. Namibia (84) at Kimberley
10 wickets	South Africa (109-0) vs. Bangladesh (108) at Bloemfontein
10 wickets	Sri Lanka (126-0) vs. Bangladesh (124) at Pietermaritzburg
10 wickets	South Africa (142-0) vs. Kenya (140) at Potchefstroom

LOWEST VICTORY MARGINS

Tied match	Sri Lanka (268-9) vs. South Africa (229-6) at Durban
3 runs	West Indies (278-5) vs. South Africa (275-9) at Cape Town
6 runs	Sri Lanka (228-6) vs. West Indies (222-9) at Cape Town
2 wickets	Australia (208-8) vs. England (204-8) at Port Elizabeth

LEADING RUN SCORERS

673 (average 61.18)	Sachin Tendulkar (India)
465 (average 58.13)	Sourav Ganguly (India)
415 (average 51.87)	Ricky Ponting (Australia)
408 (average 40.80)	Adam Gilchrist (Australia)

HIGHEST SCORERS

172*	Craig Wishart	Zimbabwe vs. Namibia at Harare
152	Sachin Tendulkar	India vs. Namibia at Pietermaritzburg
143*	Andrew Symonds	Australia vs. Pakistan at Johannesburg
143	Herschelle Gibbs	South Africa vs. New Zealand at Johannesburg
141	Scott Styris	New Zealand vs. Sri Lanka at Bloemfontein
140*	Ricky Ponting	Australia vs. India at Johannesburg

CENTURIES

Twenty-one

LEADING WICKET TAKERS

23 (average 14.39)	Chaminda Vaas (Sri Lanka)
22 (average 17.91)	Brett Lee (Australia)
21 (average 14.76)	Glenn McGrath (Australia)

BEST BOWLING PERFORMANCES

7-4-15-7	Glenn McGrath	Australia vs. Namibia at Potchefstroom
10-0-20-7	Andy Bichel	Australia vs. England at Port Elizabeth
10-2-23-6	Ashish Nehra	India vs. England at Durban.
10-2-23-6	Shane Bond	New Zealand vs. Australia at Port Elizabeth.
9.1-2-25-6	Chaminda Vaas	Sri Lanka vs. Bangladesh at Pietermaritzburg

FIVE WICKETS IN AN INNINGS
Twelve

		HIGHEST PARTNERSHIPS FOR EACH WICKET		
1	153	Sachin Tendulkar & Virender Sehwag	Ind. vs. SL	Johannesburg
2	244	Sachin Tendulkar & Sourav Ganguly	Ind. vs. Nam.	Pietermaritzburg
3	234*	Ricky Ponting & Damien Martyn	Aus. vs. Ind.	Johannesburg
4	152	Marvan Atapattu & Aravinda de Silva	SL vs. SA	Durban
5	118*	Sourav Ganguly & Yuvraj Singh	Ind. vs. Ken.	Cape Town
6	90	Alec Stewart & Andrew Flintoff	Eng. vs. Aus.	Port Elizabeth
7	98	Ramnaresh Sarwan & Ridley Jacobs	WI vs. NZ	Port Elizabeth
8	97	Michael Bevan & Andy Bichel	Aus. vs. NZ	Port Elizabeth
9	73*	Michael Bevan & Andy Bichel	Aus. vs. Eng.	Port Elizabeth
10	54	Saqlain Mushtaq & Shoaib Akhtar	Pak. vs. Eng.	Cape Town

Australia's Gary Gilmour only appeared in five ODIs, but is one of only two bowlers to take five wickets in successive World Cup matches. (PA Images)

A nanosecond from disaster. In the first World Cup final, Roy Fredericks (West Indies), would shortly become the first batsman dismissed hit wicket in ODIs. (PA Images)

Viv Richards made an imperious, unbeaten 138 in the 1979 final against England at Lord's. (PA Images)

West Indies secured consecutive World Cup trophies with a 92-run victory over England. (PA Images)

Balwinder Sandhu's early dismissal of Gordon Greenidge led to India triumphing over holders, West Indies in 1983 after scoring only 183. (PA Images)

Winston Davis, here bowling Dennis Lillee at Headingley in 1983, became the first bowler to take seven wickets in an ODI. (PA Images)

Australia's first World Cup triumph in 1987 was sealed at Calcutta's Eden Gardens, beating England by just seven runs. (Getty Images)

England's most successful World Cup batsman, Graham Gooch, famously swept his way to 115 against India in the 1987 semi-final. (Getty Images)

Imran Khan's Pakistan found form later in the 1992 tournament to lift the trophy. (PA Images)

LOWEST VICTORY MARGINS

Tied match	Sri Lanka (268-9) vs. South Africa (229-6) at Durban
3 runs	West Indies (278-5) vs. South Africa (275-9) at Cape Town
6 runs	Sri Lanka (228-6) vs. West Indies (222-9) at Cape Town
2 wickets	Australia (208-8) vs. England (204-8) at Port Elizabeth

LEADING RUN SCORERS

673 (average 61.18)	Sachin Tendulkar (India)
465 (average 58.13)	Sourav Ganguly (India)
415 (average 51.87)	Ricky Ponting (Australia)
408 (average 40.80)	Adam Gilchrist (Australia)

HIGHEST SCORERS

172*	Craig Wishart	Zimbabwe vs. Namibia at Harare
152	Sachin Tendulkar	India vs. Namibia at Pietermaritzburg
143*	Andrew Symonds	Australia vs. Pakistan at Johannesburg
143	Herschelle Gibbs	South Africa vs. New Zealand at Johannesburg
141	Scott Styris	New Zealand vs. Sri Lanka at Bloemfontein
140*	Ricky Ponting	Australia vs. India at Johannesburg

CENTURIES

Twenty-one

LEADING WICKET TAKERS

23 (average 14.39)	Chaminda Vaas (Sri Lanka)
22 (average 17.91)	Brett Lee (Australia)
21 (average 14.76)	Glenn McGrath (Australia)

BEST BOWLING PERFORMANCES

7-4-15-7	Glenn McGrath	Australia vs. Namibia at Potchefstroom
10-0-20-7	Andy Bichel	Australia vs. England at Port Elizabeth
10-2-23-6	Ashish Nehra	India vs. England at Durban.
10-2-23-6	Shane Bond	New Zealand vs. Australia at Port Elizabeth.
9.1-2-25-6	Chaminda Vaas	Sri Lanka vs. Bangladesh at Pietermaritzburg

FIVE WICKETS IN AN INNINGS
Twelve

HIGHEST PARTNERSHIPS FOR EACH WICKET				
1	153	Sachin Tendulkar & Virender Sehwag	Ind. vs. SL	Johannesburg
2	244	Sachin Tendulkar & Sourav Ganguly	Ind. vs. Nam.	Pietermaritzburg
3	234*	Ricky Ponting & Damien Martyn	Aus. vs. Ind.	Johannesburg
4	152	Marvan Atapattu & Aravinda de Silva	SL vs. SA	Durban
5	118*	Sourav Ganguly & Yuvraj Singh	Ind. vs. Ken.	Cape Town
6	90	Alec Stewart & Andrew Flintoff	Eng. vs. Aus.	Port Elizabeth
7	98	Ramnaresh Sarwan & Ridley Jacobs	WI vs. NZ	Port Elizabeth
8	97	Michael Bevan & Andy Bichel	Aus. vs. NZ	Port Elizabeth
9	73*	Michael Bevan & Andy Bichel	Aus. vs. Eng.	Port Elizabeth
10	54	Saqlain Mushtaq & Shoaib Akhtar	Pak. vs. Eng.	Cape Town

Ian Botham has been England's most successful World Cup all-rounder. (PA Images)

Arjuna Ranatunga led Sri Lanka to their 1996 World Cup triumph over Australia at Lahore. (PA Images)

In addition to his fine World Cup record, Sri Lanka's Sanath Jayasuriya had a memorable 1996 tournament with some brutal batting displays. (PA Images)

Kenya's Steve Tikolo had a fine World Cup career and played in five tournaments, the most by an Associate player (along with fellow countryman, Thomas Odoyo). (PA Images)

South Africa's Lance Klusener was the man of the moment and tournament with both bat and ball in 1999. (PA Images)

Above: Australia's Andy Bichel performed memorably with bat and ball in matches at Port Elizabeth in 2003. (Reuters)

Left: The World Cup's most successful captain, Ricky Ponting, added a century in the 2003 final against India to secure Australia's third triumph. (Reuters)

Australian Glenn McGrath was the 2007 Man of the Tournament and is the leading wicket-taker in World Cup history. (Reuters)

India were hastened to an early exit from the 2007 tournament after defeat to Bangladesh in their first match. (Reuters)

Mahendra Singh Dhoni's unbeaten 91 in the 2011 final saw India to a famous victory on home turf at Mumbai. (Reuters)

Sachin Tendulkar's sixth World Cup tournament saw the competition's most prolific batsman pick up his first winner's medal. (Alamy)

Lasith Malinga, seen bowling here in 2015, is the only bowler to take two World Cup hat-tricks. (Alamy)

Despite losing to Australia, Brendon McCullum saw New Zealand to their first World Cup final in 2015 after six semi-final defeats since 1975. (Alamy)

2007

The ICC Cricket World Cup 2007 was the first to be held in the West Indies. Although it contained marginally fewer matches than the 2003 event, there were two more teams involved taking the number to sixteen. The ten Test playing countries were joined by six Associate ICC Members from which Bermuda and Ireland made their first World Cup appearances.

Eight venues were used with each hosting a minimum of six matches with Saint Lucia's ground at Gros Islet and Jamaica's Sabina Park both hosting seven including a semi-final each. The Kensington Oval in Bridgetown, Barbados, also held seven including the final on 28 April. New stadia were built but some were not always easy to reach being out of the centre and a further difficulty which affected the organisers was the high price of tickets which deterred some of the locals from attending. Stringent entrance regulations for spectators in the earlier part of the competition were also deemed unhelpful but these were later relaxed and the familiar Caribbean revelry was able to be seen.

In all, the tournament required forty-seven days to complete despite a reduction of three games on the 2003 tournament. Four groups of four played each other with the top two from each group going through to a new Super Eight stage. This second, round-robin stage meant each side playing six further matches not seven with the two winners from the original groups not playing each other again. There were in some cases lengthy waits between matches for some countries.

Pakistan and India were expected to do well but, in an initial group stage of just three matches, an early loss could lead to a premature exit from the tournament. Pakistan made a poor start with a 54-run defeat to the hosts in Jamaica and their surprise elimination came in their very next match when they were dismissed for just 132 by Ireland and lost narrowly by three wickets.

If the early round matches had been noticeable by a lack of locals, a large Irish contingent had come to Jamaica and been delighted by their side's exciting tie with Zimbabwe – only the third in World Cup history – before their surprise defeat of Pakistan, also at Kingston. The Irish team performed heroically throughout the competition.

The Pakistan and Ireland match will be remembered for the subsequent and sudden death of the Pakistan coach, Bob Woolmer, in his room at the Jamaica Pegasus Hotel in Kingston. It was initially reported that the Pakistan coach had succumbed to a heart attack only for the Jamaican police to launch a murder investigation four days later. Almost six weeks after the World Cup had finished, an announcement was made that Woolmer had died of natural causes, but his death left a deep pall over the tournament.

India played their first-round games in Port of Spain, the capital of Trinidad and Tobago. Choosing to bat first against Bangladesh, they could only muster 191 after an impressive bowling performance by Bangladesh who went on to record a fine five-wicket victory with three of their batsmen passing fifty. India's defeat acted as a prelude to a poor tournament despite their setting the World Cup's highest total at that stage of 413 for five and a then record victory by 257 runs against Bermuda. Defeat against Sri Lanka in their last group match meant an unexpected and early departure home.

Bangladesh qualified in second place behind Sri Lanka who won their three games with resounding victories.

Bermuda would not greatly trouble their three opponents at Port of Spain, but they did contain one of the World Cup's legendary figures in the almost 20-stone Dwayne Leverock. A decent enough bowler to dismiss Kevin Pietersen (making his World Cup debut) in a practice match, Leverock is chiefly remembered for taking a superlative slip catch to dismiss India's Robin Uthappa. The ensuing celebrations made for one of the World Cup's most enduring scenes.

Australia came into the competition having not lost a World Cup match in the twenty-first century but, more recently, had lost several of their previous matches before the World Cup started. If other countries sensed an opportunity, it failed to materialise as Australia continued to impressively dominate relentlessly throughout the competition.

They ran up 377 for six against South Africa at Basseterre in a match which beat the previous highest World Cup match aggregate between Sri Lanka and Kenya in 1996, by 19 runs.

South Africa also qualified for the Super Six stage behind Australia. Herschelle Gibbs made a spectacular start to his and South Africa's campaign by becoming the third player yet first in an international match to score six sixes in an over from Daan van Bunge. Jacques Kallis also plundered the fairly short boundaries in his unbeaten 128 in the game against the Netherlands.

New Zealand and England qualified in Group C at the expense of Kenya, who could not match the form which made them semi-finalists in 2003, and Canada for whom John Davison could not repeat his heroics of 2003 despite a fifty against New Zealand. England had once again only beaten the Associate nations to qualify whilst New Zealand, in winning all three games including the defeat of England, qualified top. England's campaign had started more spectacularly in the media and off the St.Lucian coast with the notorious night-trip for which Andrew Flintoff lost his vice-captaincy position following his part in taking a pedalo into the sea. A happier occasion for Flintoff came five years later when, in raising money for charity, he took to the calmer waters of the Serpentine in Hyde Park with fellow cricketer, Steve Harmison, and set the world record for a 100m pedalo race.

Group D saw West Indies qualify in first place after wins in all three games. Ireland sprung a surprise after their tie with Zimbabwe and defeat of Pakistan by qualifying ahead of Pakistan and Zimbabwe. After Woolmer's death, Pakistan, despite their early exit, made their highest-ever World Cup total of 349 against Zimbabwe.

The Super Eight stage started with Sri Lanka, Australia, West Indies and New Zealand taking forward the two points from their result against their group's other qualifier whilst England, Ireland, South Africa and Bangladesh qualified but with no further points accrued from the group stage.

Australia continued their dominance with a further six straight wins by 103 runs, 10 wickets, seven wickets, nine wickets, seven wickets and then ruthlessly beating New Zealand by 215 runs, at that time a World Cup record for the biggest runs victory over a fellow Test nation. Matthew Hayden added two further centuries to the one he scored earlier in the competition against South Africa en route to scoring 659 runs in the competition, just 14 behind Tendulkar's 2003 record. Eventual Player of the Tournament, Glenn McGrath, continued his fine run despite not always opening the bowling.

South Africa needed only 210 to beat Sri Lanka in their first game of the second stage and reached comparative comfort at 206 for five. Lasith Malinga, however, managed not only a hat-trick but a further wicket with his next ball but, ultimately, South Africa squeezed home by one wicket. Despite winning their next match against Ireland, they stumbled against Bangladesh and New Zealand but managed to qualify for the knock-out stage.

Despite a spirited performance by Ireland in Guyana, England beat them by 48 runs, but England could only win three of their six matches despite centuries for Pietersen against Australia and West Indies. They needed 236 to beat Sri Lanka and seemed unlikely to challenge after losing their sixth wicket with 103 still needed. An 87-run seventh wicket partnership between Ravi Bopara and Paul Nixon took the match to the last ball but Bopara was bowled by Fernando with England two short.

Pietersen's 104 and Ian Bell's 77 could only set Australia 248 as eight players failed to reach double figures. Captain and top-scorer Ricky Ponting's 86 saw Australia to their sixth consecutive win of the competition. Despite a tense win against Bangladesh requiring just 144, England's campaign finished ignominiously with a nine-wicket defeat to South Africa after managing just 154 with the bat and losing with 30.4 balls remaining. Pietersen's hundred salvaged an exciting match against West Indies at Bridgetown and they made the 301 target with the last pair in and with only one ball remaining. At that stage, their total was the second highest successful World Cup chase behind Sri Lanka's 313 for seven against Zimbabwe at New Plymouth in 1992. The match also brought the close to Brian Lara's supreme international career. Amongst over 22,000 international runs, Lara currently sits fourth in World Cup batting records with 1225 runs.

The hosts did not progress further, losing their first four matches in the Super Eights and could only muster one win against Bangladesh. All sides registered at least one win in this second stage and Bangladesh's was a fine won over South Africa but their interest in the competition did not extend beyond the Super Eight stage.

Ireland's sole win was against Bangladesh making it the eleventh win for Associate Members over Test playing countries. Ireland's batting, though, could only muster 77 against Sri Lanka, 91 against Australia and 134 against New Zealand. They had shown great promise in their first World Cup appearance.

Despite their exciting match but narrow loss to South Africa, Sri Lanka nonetheless recorded four wins in qualifying for the semi-finals. Sanath Jayasuriya, playing in his fifth but last World Cup, enjoyed a fine series which included two centuries and two further fifties. His 115 against West Indies comfortably saw off the host's challenge. Captain Mahela Jayawardene also enjoyed an impressive series with 548 runs – the most by a Sri Lankan batsman in a World Cup tournament – as did Muttiah Muralitharan. His 23 wickets in the 2007 competition is joint-most for Sri Lanka with Chaminda Vaas (in 2003).

New Zealand joined Australia, Sri Lanka and South Africa in the semi-finals despite their heavy defeat to Australia in their last Super Eight match. Their four wins included their first three in the second stage and their defeat of South Africa in a low-scoring game in Grenada saw them through to their fifth World Cup semi-final. Scott Styris's excellent all-round series with 499 runs and economical bowling made him an important contributor. His four for 43 helped win the game against Bangladesh although his unbeaten 111 against Sri Lanka at Grenada was in a losing cause.

The first semi-final saw Sri Lanka pitted against New Zealand at Kingston. A far from full Sabina Park witnessed a very fine century from Sri Lankan captain Jayawardene who had won the toss and elected to bat. His unbeaten 115 took his side to a decent 289 for five after they were languishing slightly at 187 after 40 overs.

Five New Zealand batsmen made starts but none reached 50 as Muralitharan dismantled their chase with four cheap wickets. Despite a 73-run partnership between Styris and Peter Fulton, the innings swiftly subsided and it was only a tenth-wicket partnership of 59 between James Franklin and Jeetan Patel which lifted the total over 200. Once again, New Zealand were the vanquished team whilst Sri Lanka entered their second final.

The second semi-final between defending champions, Australia, and South Africa at St. Lucia's Beausejour stadium was no less close. South Africa's first visit to the St. Lucia stadium did not turn out to be a nice stay for them as, on winning the toss, their batsmen's aggressive starts left them reeling at 27 for five. Justin Kemp and Gibbs made reasonable contributions but Shaun Tait and McGrath with four and three wickets ended the innings at just 149.

Gilchrist's early departure may have given South Africa heart and hope, but Hayden's 41 saw him past 600 runs for the tournament. Michael Clarke's undefeated 60 saw Australia through to their sixth World Cup final with 18.3 overs remaining.

Much did not go to plan during the final. Rain delayed the start by two-and-three-quarter hours which reduced each innings from 50 to 38 overs. Australia, on winning the toss, made a superlative start through Hayden but predominantly Gilchrist and although after ten overs the score was only 46, the rate increased thereafter and after Gilchrist had survived a hard chance.

Hayden's impressive tournament ended with 38 at 172 with Gilchrist well past his century, the fifth such made in a final. Although he fell one short of 150, it is still the highest in a final and the only one made by a wicket-keeper. It led to an imposing total of 281 for four in their 38 overs.

Gilchrist was soon in the action again catching Upul Tharanga off Nathan Bracken's bowling with just seven on the board. However, a spirited response came through Jayasuriya and Kumar Sangakkara who both made impressive fifties but, after both had been dismissed, the rain returned and the players again had to leave the field. On the resumption, the Sri Lankan target was adjusted to 269 from 36 overs. The Sri Lankan batsmen tried their hardest, but wickets fell and with no floodlights and the light failing, their later-order batsmen accepted the light when 63 runs from three overs were required.

Confusion reigned as Australia celebrated their fourth World Cup success and third in a row, but the officials thought that the three remaining overs had still to be bowled. After 20 overs of the Sri Lankan innings had been bowled, a result would stand on the day but, in near darkness, the players traipsed out again to bowl the three overs to finally complete the tournament. Ricky Ponting had hoped that the retiring Glenn McGrath would bowl the final over as a salute to his outstanding international performances since 1993. Ultimately, safety decreed that the overs be bowled by the spinners.

2007 MISCELLANY

- Five of the top ten heaviest runs defeats took place in the 2007 competition.
- The only bowlers who took five wickets in an innings were from South Africa. Details are given in the statistics section below.
- Ireland's Jeremy Bray became the second player from a non-Test playing nation to score a century on World Cup debut. Andy Flower achieved the feat in 1992 against Sri Lanka (which was his first ODI also). Bray also became the fourth Associate Member player to score a century against a Test playing country following Dave Houghton (Zimbabwe vs. New Zealand in 1987), Flower and John Davison (Canada vs West Indies in 2003).
- Australian bowler, Nathan Bracken, did not bat once in the ten games he played, a World Cup record.

2007 STATISTICS

HIGHEST TOTALS	
413 for 5 in 50 overs	India vs. Bermuda at Port of Spain
377 for 6 in 50 overs	Australia vs. South Africa at Basseterre
363 for 5 in 50 overs	New Zealand vs. Canada at Gros Islet
358 for 5 in 50 overs	Australia vs. Netherlands at Basseterre
356 for 4 in 50 overs	South Africa vs. West Indies at St George's

LOWEST COMPLETED TOTALS	
77 in 27.4 overs	Ireland vs. Sri Lanka at St. George's
78 in 24.4 overs	Bermuda vs. Sri Lanka at Port of Spain
91 in 30 overs	Ireland vs. Australia at Bridgetown
99 in 19.1 overs	Zimbabwe vs. Pakistan at Kingston

HIGHEST MATCH AGGREGATES	
671 for 16 wickets	Australia (377-6) vs. South Africa (294) at Basseterre
645 for 13 wickets	South Africa (356-4) vs. West Indies (289-9) at St. George's
612 for 14 wickets	New Zealand (363-5) vs. Canada (249-9) at Gros Islet
601 for 19 wickets	West Indies (300) vs. England (301-9) at Bridgetown

LOWEST MATCH AGGREGATES WITH RESULTS	
158 for 12 wickets	Ireland (77) vs. Sri Lanka (81-2) at St. George's
183 for 11 wickets	Ireland (91) vs. Australia (92-1) at Bridgetown
190 for 12 wickets	Bermuda (94-9) vs. Bangladesh (96-3) at Port of Spain

BIGGEST VICTORY MARGINS	
257 runs	India (413-5) vs. Bermuda (156) at Port of Spain
243 runs	Sri Lanka (321-6) vs. Bermuda (78) at Port of Spain
229 runs	Australia (358-5) vs. Netherlands (129) at Basseterre
221 runs	South Africa (353-3) vs. Netherlands (132-9) at Basseterre
10 wickets	Australia (106-0) vs. Bangladesh (104-6) at North Sound

LOWEST VICTORY MARGINS	
Tied match	Ireland (221-9) vs. Zimbabwe (221) at Kingston
2 runs	Sri Lanka (235) vs. England (233-8) at North Sound
1 wicket	South Africa (212-9) vs. Sri Lanka (209) at Providence
1 wicket	England (301-9) vs. West Indies (300) at Bridgetown

LEADING RUN SCORERS	
659 (average 73.22)	Matthew Hayden (Australia)
548 (average 60.89)	Mahela Jayawardene (Sri Lanka)
539 (average 67.38)	Ricky Ponting (Australia)
499 (average 83.17)	Scott Styris (New Zealand)

HIGHEST SCORES		
160	Imran Nazir	Pakistan vs. Zimbabwe at Kingston
158	Matthew Hayden	Australia vs. West Indies at North Sound
149	Adam Gilchrist	Australia vs. Sri Lanka at Bridgetown
146	Abraham de Villiers	South Africa vs. West Indies at St. George's

CENTURIES
Twenty

LEADING WICKET TAKERS

26 (average 13.73)	Glenn McGrath (Australia)
23 (average 15.26)	Muttiah Muralitharan (Sri Lanka)
23 (average 20.30)	Shaun Tait (Australia)
21 (average 15.81)	Brad Hogg (Australia)

BEST BOWLING PERFORMANCES

10-2-18-5	Andrew Hall	South Africa vs. England at Bridgetown
10-1-39-5	Charl Langeveldt	South Africa vs. Sri Lanka at Providence
10-1-45-5	Andre Nel	South Africa vs. Bangladesh at Providence

FIVE WICKETS IN AN INNINGS

Three

HIGHEST PARTNERSHIPS FOR EACH WICKET

1	172	Adam Gilchrist & Matthew Hayden	Aus. vs. SL	Bridgetown
2	202	Sourav Ganguly & Virender Sehwag	Ind. vs. Ber.	Port of Spain
3	183	Sanath Jayasuriya & Mahela Jayawardene	SL vs. WI	Providence
4	204	Michael Clarke & Brad Hodge	Aus. vs. Net.	Basseterre
5	138*	Scott Styris & Jacob Oram	NZ vs. Eng.	Gros Islet
6	97	Tillakaratne Dilshan & Russel Arnold	SL vs. SA	Providence
7	87	Ravi Bopara & Paul Nixon	Eng. vs. SL	North Sound
8	71*	Paul Nixon & Liam Plunkett	Eng. vs. NZ	Gros Islet
	71	Brendon McCullum & James Franklin	NZ vs. Ire.	Providence
9	44	David Hemp & Dwayne Leverock	Ber. vs. Ind.	Port of Spain
10	59	James Franklin & Jeetan Patel	NZ vs. SL	Kingston

2011

The ICC Cricket World Cup 2011 returned to the subcontinent for the third time and the first since 1996. Three countries hosted forty-nine matches with twenty-nine being played in India, twelve in Sri Lanka and eight in Bangladesh. Pakistan had been one of the original co-hosts until April 2009 when concerns over safety were raised following the attack on Sri Lankan cricketers in their bus in Lahore. India was granted the final and one semi-final whilst Sri Lanka hosted the other semi-final.

There were two fewer sides contesting the tournament thus dropping the number to fourteen which were played between two groups of seven, each playing the other and the top four winners of each group then qualifying for the quarter-finals. Matches were again played over 50 overs per side.

A very enthusiastic opening ceremony was held in Dhaka at the Bangabandhu National Stadium two days before the first match. Games would, though, be played at the newer Sher-e-Bangla ground at Mirpur, 10 kilometres away from Dhaka city centre.

Bangladesh and India met in the first match at Dhaka and although the hosts batted spiritedly in reaching 283 for nine in the match's second innings, their neighbours had shown intent in reclaiming the World Cup having earlier reached 370 for four. Virender Sehwag had made an aggressive 140-ball 175 whilst Virat Kohli, playing in his first World Cup match, reached 100 before the innings ended.

When India had won the World Cup in 1983, it was deemed a surprise but twenty-eight years later and in a changing nation, there was far more pressure on the players to bring the trophy home. In Mahendra Singh Dhoni, they had the ideal and calm leader and whilst their progress was not always as serene as their respected wicket-keeper/batsman and leader, they did start impressively and maintained a decent level throughout the group matches and peaked at the right time.

India met England at Bangalore in a thrilling encounter which saw 676 runs scored and after the final ball had been bowled, the sides could not be separated and the World Cup saw its fourth tie. India had impressively built up 338 despite a late collapse with Tendulkar scoring another century in his record sixth World Cup but led by captain Andrew Strauss's 158, an unlikely victory for England seemed probable. Wickets, though, fell and a heroic chase could not quite seal victory. This match had been moved late on from Kolkata's Eden Gardens after construction work had deemed the ground to be not ready on time.

India maintained their victory charge against Ireland, also at Bangalore, where Yuvraj Singh, ultimately the Man of the Tournament, became the first player ever to score fifty and take five wickets in a World Cup match. India, however, blew a fine position against South Africa after losing their last nine wickets for just 29 and conceding 16 in the final over of the South African innings to go down by three wickets. Tendulkar's record sixth and final World Cup century was therefore in a losing cause.

Co-hosts Bangladesh, who played all their matches in Dhaka and Chittagong, successfully defended 205 against Ireland but let themselves down against West Indies capitulating for just 58, the lowest World Cup total by a Test-playing country. Some fans set upon the West Indian bus after the match, but later more restrained ones issued apologies. Against England in Chittagong, they faced a target of 226 and had a fine start requiring 71 with seven wickets remaining. A rapid collapse left them reeling but a restrained innings from Mahmudullah and an energetic one from Shafiul Islam saw Bangladesh home by two wickets. Although they defeated Netherlands, a 206-run defeat and a dismissal for just 78 against South Africa left them out of contention for the knock-out stage.

England had an eventful tournament. After conceding 292 to Netherlands, they managed to bat more impressively and end any hopes of a giant-killing with a six-wicket victory. The dramatic tie in Bangalore was followed by an even more remarkable game at the same ground less than a week later when they stumbled to a three-wicket defeat against Ireland after failing to defend 328. A far-from packed venue witnessed a triumphant Irish comeback and a remarkable onslaught by Kevin O'Brien who made very considerably the quickest-ever World Cup century in just 50 balls. England captain Strauss was thus left with a much unwanted birthday present.

In Chennai, England, after totals of 296, 338 and 327 in their first three matches, only managed 171 against South Africa. It proved sufficient with their opponents reaching just 165 in return after requiring 48 with seven wickets in hand. After the unhelpful loss to Bangladesh, England needed victory against West Indies to remain in the competition. Chennai's M.A.Chidambaram stadium again saw them come up trumps in a close tussle where they managed to defend 243. Six West Indian wickets had been lost for 150 before a 72-run partnership between Sarwan and Russell had put West Indies firmly back in contention. It did not happen and England won by 18 runs with over five overs remaining.

From their 2007 squad, England had lost Ed Joyce to his native Ireland but Eoin Morgan would make the transition in the opposite direction.

South Africa, despite the loss to England, topped the group with five victories. Impressive batting from A.B. de Villiers with hundreds in the first two matches against West Indies and Netherlands saw them make a decent start to their campaign before the aberration against England. With India on 267 for one at Nagpur, there might have been cause for concern but, in restricting their opponents to 296, they were set a lower target than seemed likely and ultimately came through in the last over. Jean-Paul Duminy became only the second player to be dismissed for 99 in the World Cup but his innings led to an easy victory against Ireland at a now-ready Eden Gardens. The thrashing of Bangladesh in Dhaka led to the fifth of their six round group matches.

Although they could not quite repeat their heroics of 2007 and did not reach the quarter-finals in 2011, Ireland still showcased their talents. The rousing victory over England at Bangalore added to their list of impressive victories over Test playing nations and indeed, in achieving 328, theirs is the highest successful chase in the World Cup. They put in a further spirited performance against India at Bangalore and gave West Indies a few anxious moments at Mohali before losing by 44 runs. A heavy defeat against South Africa was followed by a further successful chase against Netherlands at Kolkata where they comfortably made the 307-target aided by Paul Stirling's hundred.

One area where Ireland did not excel, though, was in the Decision Review System where, of eleven challenges, none was overturned. In fact, due to a little-realised rule, decisions could be overturned if the batsman was more than 2.5 metres in front of the crease. This became noticed during the tense tie between India and England with Ian Bell benefiting from the clause.

Netherlands may have returned home without a win but, despite heavy defeats against South Africa and West Indies where they lost by over 200 runs in each game, they put together some decent performances. Essex's Ryan ten Doeschate started the tournament with a fine 119 against England and hit a further hundred against Ireland at Kolkata in their last game. In between, he made an unbeaten 53 against Bangladesh before running out of partners.

West Indies qualified in fourth place but might have reached a higher place after missing opportunities in their last two matches to defeat England and India, both at Chennai. Although the 80-run defeat against India was conclusive, they had reached 154 for three in search of 269 only to go down for 188. One highlight was Kemar Roach's hat-trick against Netherlands, the first by a West Indian in the World Cup.

In Group A, New Zealand arrived after the devastating earthquake in Christchurch but immediately made light work of Kenya in their first game. Dismissing them for 69, New Zealand needed just eight overs to record a ten-wicket victory in Chennai. Despite a heavy defeat to Australia, they recorded a further ten-wicket win over Zimbabwe before very easily seeing off Pakistan in Pallekele. Ross Taylor became the first and to date only player to record a birthday World Cup century. Brendon McCullum hit a century in his side's 97-run win over Canada at Mumbai and forged useful opening partnerships throughout the group stage with Martin Guptill. Despite a hefty loss to Sri Lanka, they still qualified in fourth place.

Australia arrived in the sub-continent having not lost a World Cup match since 1999 and won four of their first five matches. Their match against Sri Lanka in the middle of this run was abandoned after torrential rain ensured that there would be no result between the previous tournament's finalists. Despite their victories, some of the underdogs performed creditably against the defending champions.

Zimbabwe restricted them to 262 at Ahmedabad whilst Kenya, chasing 325, managed a praiseworthy 264 for six in their 50 overs. Collins Obuya, whose bowling had been influential in the 2003 tournament, had made himself into a respectable batsman after his bowling faltered and he narrowly failed to become the first Kenyan to score a World Cup century finishing on 98 not out.

Canada also managed to score 211 against them before succumbing by seven wickets at Bangalore. Mitchell Johnson started impressively with four wickets in each of the first two matches whilst Jason Krejza made a comeback to the country where he had started his Test career so spectacularly with twelve wickets at Nagpur. He could not repeat his successes and went wicketless in the game against New Zealand on the same ground.

Although many of Australia's biggest names had retired, Ricky Ponting was still in charge but struggling with the bat. Colombo's R. Premadasa Stadium did, after almost twelve years, see Australia's first defeat. Although Australia had beaten them twice in the interim period including the 1999 final, it was Pakistan (who had been the team to defeat them last) who inflicted defeat in the last group match. Australia's record of going undefeated through 34 matches is over three times greater than any other country's such streak. The implications of this match were greater as it meant that Pakistan went through to the quarter-finals top of Group A (and would play West Indies) whilst Australia, in third place, would meet India.

Kenya had little to cheer and their batting remained weak. After the debacle against New Zealand, they could manage only 112 against Pakistan, 142 against Sri Lanka and 147 against Zimbabwe. Although they conceded 324 to Australia, their batting in their last match would prove to be their most praiseworthy. In the battle of the Associate Members, they lost by five wickets to Canada. Two sets of brothers, Collins and David Obuya and James Ngoche and Nehemiah Odhiambo, would represent Kenya in three of their matches and after sterling service to his country, Steve Tikolo finished his five tournament, World Cup career.

Only slightly before their arrival in India did Canada know that they could field their strongest side after three of their players, all born in Pakistan, were ultimately granted visas. They fared little better than Kenya, managing only 122 against Sri Lanka, 123 against Zimbabwe and 138 against Pakistan. In fact, they had given themselves a chance of a major upset against Pakistan after bowling the match favourites out for just 184.

They did record a win against Kenya at Delhi chasing 199 largely through Jimmy Hansra's 70 and wicket-keeper/batsman and captain Ashish Bagai's unbeaten 64. Their batting also came good against New Zealand at Mumbai where they managed 261 for nine but this was still 97 runs short of their target. Despite batting comparatively well against Australia, their campaign ended with a seven-wicket defeat.

In topping Group A, Pakistan lost just one game to New Zealand. At times, their scorecards made for bewildering reading. In their first game against Kenya, only four batsmen reached double-figures but those made fifties as Pakistan scored 317 for seven aided by a liberal helping of extras. They could only manage 184 against Canada but their bowlers ensured that there was no upset and after their defeat to New Zealand, they toppled Zimbabwe and Australia. Captain Shahid Afridi's bowling included two five-wicket hauls whilst the more experienced Misbah-ul-Haq and Younis Khan chipped in with useful runs.

Sri Lanka might have topped the group but for the rains in Colombo against Australia. Their performance nonetheless was impressive with four of their batsmen scoring centuries in the group stage. Their only defeat came against Pakistan in Colombo where they failed by only 11 runs to overhaul Pakistan's 277 for seven. They played just one group match outside their home country and easily overcame New Zealand at Mumbai with Sangakkara and Jayawardene leading the way with a 145-run partnership. Lasith Malinga became the first bowler to record two World Cup hat-tricks in the match against Kenya.

An astonishing performance by Tillakaratne Dilshan saw off Zimbabwe in Pallekele. Dilshan and Upul Tharanga opened with a record World Cup first-wicket partnership of 282 before Dilshan, who had scored 144, finished the match with four wickets for four runs in three overs.

Zimbabwe, still not playing Test cricket although a return took place within five months of the World Cup ending, had impressive wins against Canada and Kenya and were indebted to Craig Ervine predominantly although Tatenda Taibu and Brendan Taylor had their moments with the bat as did left-arm spinner, Ray Price, with the ball who often opened the bowling. Taibu shortly afterwards retired from cricket to work for the church.

The knock-out stage arrived with West Indies meeting Pakistan in Dhaka; India taking on Australia at Ahmedabad; New Zealand facing South Africa also at Dhaka and England hoping for a better result in a repeat of their 1996 quarter-final against Sri Lanka, this time at Colombo.

West Indies elected to bat first against Pakistan but could only manage 112, a total which their opponents knocked off with almost 30 overs remaining and without losing a wicket. Afridi continued his fine bowling with a further four wickets.

India contested a fine match against Australia where Ponting's return to form led to his fifth – and final – World Cup century. Aided by wicket-keeper Brad Haddin's fifty and a late flourish from David Hussey, Australia set India a respectable target of 261. Three fifties were scored but wickets fell at inappropriate times for the home team but ultimately Yuvraj and Suresh Raina took India home by five wickets with fourteen balls remaining. Australia's domination was thus ended and the tenth World Cup was guaranteed a different victor from the previous three.

New Zealand was indebted to 83 from Jesse Ryder in reaching 221 for eight against South Africa. In an at times fractious contest, South Africa had reached a position of some strength only for a woeful collapse see them lose six wickets for only 38 runs and ultimately end their interest in a tournament prematurely again.

England's hopes did not materialise in Colombo. Only Jonathan Trott, who enjoyed a good series with the bat, with 86 and a fifty from Morgan could lift England to 229 for six. Their target only served for Tharanga and Dilshan to add a further double-century opening partnership and, in not being parted, inflict a ten-wicket defeat upon England. Their 231 partnership remains the largest by a World Cup opening pair batting second and winning.

Sri Lanka therefore played New Zealand and India would take on Pakistan, both hosts playing in their own countries. Although New Zealand made a reasonable if cautious start, a late-order collapse saw them bowled out without facing their allocation of overs and again they could only offer 218 for Sri Lanka to reach their second successive and third final in all.

Although New Zealand had a surge late on, the start given Sri Lanka by Dilshan and Sangakkara meant that a five-wicket was achieved leaving New Zealand vanquished for the sixth occasion in a semi-final.

India and Pakistan met at Mohali in the fifth World Cup meeting between the teams with India yet to lose to their neighbours. Never, though, had they met at such a late stage in the World Cup, the 1996 tournament quarter-final at Bangalore being the only time in the knock-out stage when they had done so.

Although there were contributions and starts from five Indian batsmen, it was Tendulkar's 85 which took India as far as 260 when their overs finished. Indian fans and players were grateful for their hero being dropped four times and surviving a DRS appeal en route to his twenty-first score of 50 or more in the World Cup. Pakistan, like New Zealand, were contesting their sixth semi-final and were grateful to Wahab Riaz whose five for 46 made him the first Pakistani bowler to take five wickets in a World Cup semi-final.

Seven of the first eight Pakistani batsmen reached double figures but only Misbah-ul-Haq reached 50 as wickets fell at reasonably regular intervals. All Indian bowlers shared the wickets but Misbah's dismissal meant that India yet again were victorious and although there were subsequent rumours about match-fixing in the game, at the time Pakistan's innings ended India's fans were delighted that their country had a chance to win their second World Cup and first on home soil.

Mumbai's Wankhede's stadium held 42,000 spectators for the India and Sri Lanka final. Around a billion others in India watched through other means. Sri Lanka made as many as four changes and they hoped that the retiring Muttiah Muralitharan would have one last hurrah. There was confusion at the toss resulting in it having to be taken again. Won by Sangakkara, Sri Lanka batted first but quickly lost Tharanga to a fine slip catch by Sehwag.

Tharanga's loss was remedied by Dilshan, Sangakkara but, most pertinently, Jayawardene who became the sixth player to score a World Cup final century. It came in only 84 balls and after Sri Lanka found themselves in need of a late surge after losing their fifth wicket at 182 in the fortieth over, Jayawardene was able to achieve it. The final total of 274 was the fifth highest total by a side batting first and only Sri Lanka themselves had ever won a final batting second facing a total of over 200.

They were immediately buoyed further by Sehwag's second-ball dismissal. Tendulkar, in his record-equalling sixth World Cup, could not achieve a Boycott-style 100th hundred on his home ground, and was out at 31. A rescue act ensued between Gautam Gambhir and Kohli but, on the latter's dismissal, it was not the in-form Yuvraj who appeared but his captain, M.S. Dhoni, who had enjoyed an excellent tournament with his decision-making but not so much with the bat. It proved to be an inspired decision.

There would be no fairy tale for Muralitharan who did not complete his ten overs and who was carrying a slight niggle. Despite a century partnership with his captain, Gambhir was dismissed for 97 but his innings had put his side into a strong position to achieve the desired result for all their fanatical fans. When it did come, it came quickly. There would be no fairy tale hundred for the skipper either but who will forget M.S.D.'s eyes as he and a billion others watched the second ball of the forty-eighth over sail into the stands to achieve India's second World Cup victory?

2011 MISCELLANY

- Of the eleven ten-wicket results in the World Cup, four were achieved in the 2011 tournament.
- Bangalore, like Basseterre, has seen the record number of batsmen dismissed in the 90s with four.
- Pakistan's Shahid Afridi became the first captain to take five wickets in an innings twice in the World Cup. Kapil Dev is the only other captain to take five wickets in an innings.
- Kenya's Steve Tikolo's 28 World Cup appearances is the most by a non-Test playing country. His selection in five World Cup tournaments is also a record for an Associate Member country.
- The Kenyan innings against Sri Lanka saw only the second World Cup instance of two fifties being scored whilst all other nine batsmen failed to reach double figures. At The Oval in 1999, India recorded a total which included one century, one fifty but nine below double figures.
- The 2011 tournament is the only one to witness hat-tricks on successive days. Kemar Roach's hat-trick for West Indies against Netherlands on 28 February was followed on 1 March by Lasith Malinga's for Sri Lanka against Kenya.

- Mahela Jayawardene's unbeaten 103 is the only occasion of a hundred being scored by a player on the losing side in a final.
- The match aggregate of 613 for 14 wickets between Netherlands and Ireland is the highest in the World Cup between two non-Test playing countries.
- Canada's Nitish Kumar became the youngest player to appear in the World. At 16 years and 283 days, he surpassed Bangladesh's Talha Jubair who played in 2003 at 17 years and 70 days.
- Upul Tharanga and Tillakaratne Dilshan are the only openers to both score centuries in a World Cup innings. They did so twice, once for Sri Lanka against Zimbabwe at Pallekele and against England at Colombo.
- Netherlands lost four batsmen to run outs in successive matches, the first time against Bangladesh at Chittagong and then to Ireland at Kolkata.
- For the only time in a final, both captains were also the wicket-keepers.

2011 STATISTICS

HIGHEST TOTALS	
370 for 4 in 50 overs	India vs. Bangladesh at Dhaka.
358 for 6 in 50 overs	New Zealand vs. Canada at Mumbai
351 for 5 in 50 overs	South Africa vs. Netherlands at Mohali
338 for 8 in 50 overs	England vs. India at Bangalore
338 in 49.5 overs	India vs. England at Bangalore

LOWEST COMPLETED TOTALS	
58 in 18.5 overs	Bangladesh vs. West Indies at Dhaka
69 in 23.5 overs	Kenya vs. New Zealand at Chennai
78 in 28 overs	Bangladesh vs. South Africa at Dhaka

HIGHEST MATCH AGGREGATES	
676 for 18 wickets	India (338) vs. England (338-8) at Bangalore
656 for 15 wickets	England (327-8) vs. Ireland (329-7) at Bangalore
653 for 13 wickets	India (370-4) vs. Bangladesh (283-9) at Dhaka
619 for 15 wickets	New Zealand (358-6) vs. Canada (261-9) at Mumbai
613 for 14 wickets	Netherlands (306) vs. Ireland (307-4) at Kolkata

LOWEST MATCH AGGREGATES WITH RESULT	
117 for 11 wickets	Bangladesh (58) vs. West Indies (59-1) at Dhaka
141 for 10 wickets	Kenya (69) vs. New Zealand (72-0) at Chennai
225 for 10 wickets	West Indies (112) vs. Pakistan (113-0) at Dhaka

BIGGEST VICTORY MARGINS	
231 runs	South Africa (351-5) vs. Netherlands (120) at Mohali
215 runs	West Indies (330-8) vs. Netherlands (115) at Delhi
210 runs	Sri Lanka (332-7) vs. Canada (122) at Hambantota
10 wickets	New Zealand (166-0) vs. Zimbabwe (162) at Ahmedabad
10 wickets	Sri Lanka (231-0) vs. England (229-6) at Colombo
10 wickets	Pakistan (113-0) vs. West Indies (112) at Dhaka
10 wickets	New Zealand (72-0) vs. Kenya (69) at Chennai

LOWEST VICTORY MARGINS	
Tied match	India (338) vs. England (338-8) at Bangalore
6 runs	England (171) vs. South Africa (165) at Chennai
11 runs	Pakistan (277-7) vs. Sri Lanka (266-9) at Colombo
2 wickets	Bangladesh (227-8) vs. England (225) at Chittagong

LEADING RUN SCORERS	
500 (average 62.50)	Tillakaratne Dilshan (Sri Lanka)
482 (average 53.56)	Sachin Tendulkar (India)
465 (average 93.00)	Kumar Sangakkara (Sri Lanka)

HIGHEST SCORES		
175	Virender Sehwag	India vs. Bangladesh at Dhaka
158	Andrew Strauss	England vs. India at Bangalore
144	Tillakaratne Dilshan	Sri Lanka vs. Zimbabwe at Pallekele
134	Abraham de Villiers	South Africa vs. Netherlands at Mohali
133	Upul Tharanga	Sri Lanka vs. Zimbabwe at Pallekele

CENTURIES
Twenty-four

LEADING WICKET TAKERS

21 (average 12.86)	Shahid Afridi (Pakistan)
21 (average 18.76)	Zaheer Khan (India)

BEST BOWLING PERFORMANCES

8.3-0-27-6	Kemar Roach	West Indies vs. Netherlands at Delhi
7.4-0-38-6	Lasith Malinga	Sri Lanka vs. Kenya at Colombo
8-3-16-5	Shahid Afridi	Pakistan vs. Kenya at Hambantota
10-0-23-5	Shahid Afridi	Pakistan vs. Canada at Colombo

FIVE WICKETS IN AN INNINGS

Nine

HIGHEST PARTNERSHIPS FOR EACH WICKET

1	282	Upul Tharanga & Tillakaratne Dilshan	SL vs. Zim	Pallekele
2	134	Gautam Gambhir & Sachin Tendulkar	Ind. vs. Eng.	Bangalore
3	221	Hashim Amla & Abraham de Villiers	SA vs. Net.	Mohali
4	132	Ashish Bagai & Jimmy Hansra	Can. vs. Ken.	Delhi
5	121	Ryan ten Doeschate & Peter Borren	Net. vs. Ire.	Kolkata
6	162	Kevin O'Brien & Alex Cusack	Ire. vs. Eng.	Bangalore
7	85	Ross Taylor & Jacob Oram	NZ vs. Pak.	Pallekele
8	54	Neil McCullum & Daniel Vettori	NZ vs. Aus	Nagpur
9	66	Abdul Razzaq & Umar Gul	Pak. vs. NZ	Pallekele
10	23	Misbah-ul-Haq & Saeed Ajmal	Pak. vs. Ind.	Mohali
	23	Nehemiah Odhiambo & James Ngoche	Ken. vs. Zim.	Kolkata

2015

It had been confirmed that the 2015 World Cup would be held in Australia and New Zealand as far back as 2006 soon after voting had closed for the 2011 tournament. On that occasion, the Australasian bid had lost out to the Asian but, a short time afterwards, the ICC awarded the 2015 tournament to the Antipodean countries.

There was disquiet after the ICC decided that the 2015 tournament would feature only Test-playing countries but, a short time afterwards, this decision was rescinded after Ireland and other Associate Member countries registered strong disapproval and the tournament was soon confirmed as including fourteen teams which would play forty-nine matches. United Arab Emirates qualified for the first time since 1996 and Afghanistan won through to make their World Cup debut. The forty-nine matches saw twenty-six in Australia and twenty-three in New Zealand with each country using seven venues.

The tournament was notable for some breath-taking scoring by individuals and teams. Six of the top ten World Cup totals were scored in 2015 and the highest thus far achieved. The World Cup saw its first individual double century and thereby highest score, but it lasted less than a month before being antiquated from the record books. There was also the first instance of one batsman scoring four centuries and a record of thirty-eight made in the tournament.

Bowlers too held sway to a degree. Whilst Martin Snedden's concession of over 100 runs in a World Cup innings way back in 1983 was equalled by two bowlers in 2015, two other bowlers reached the top ten performances with seven and six wickets respectively.

Ireland added to their burgeoning list of defeating Test playing countries and although none of the Associate Members went beyond the pool stage (which required forty-two matches), there were some notable performances.

Australia went impressively through the group stage with just one loss and one abandoned game. Starting off against England at Melbourne, Aaron Finch's 135 took his side to 342 for nine although this might have been fewer had Chris Woakes caught him before he had scored. Steven Finn took one of the World Cup's more bizarre hat-tricks, all three dismissed batsmen attempting big shots from the final three balls of the innings. In reply, James Taylor was denied the possibility of a century after a misunderstanding by the umpire which resulted in James Anderson being given run out.

One of the matches of the tournament was against New Zealand in Auckland, the only time Australia would play outside their country. Grateful for a last-wicket partnership of 45 which took them to just 151, New Zealand captain Brendon McCullum's 24-ball 50 seemed to have ensured an early finish. Indeed, the match lasted only 55.3 overs and the New Zealand innings only 23.1 as Mitchell Starc returned six for 28. They remain the second-best World Cup bowling figures in a losing cause as New Zealand hung on to win by just one wicket.

India's 413 for five against Bermuda in 2007 was overhauled as the highest World Cup total by Australia as they managed 417 for six at Perth against Afghanistan. Three Afghan bowlers conceded 80 or more and Dawlat Zadran joined Snedden from 32 years earlier in conceding over 100. David Warner's 178 made him Australia's highest World Cup scorer and their 275-run victory became the event's largest-ever runs victory.

Their win against Sri Lanka at Sydney saw a tournament record highest aggregate, 688, as they themselves managed 376 with Glenn Maxwell becoming the third Australian centurion of the tournament at that stage.

Co-hosts New Zealand would trump Australia's with six wins in the pool stage. None of theirs were abandoned like Australia but, having won the tense yet frenetic game in Auckland, they came out on top of Pool A. Largely due to some remarkable batting from their captain, Brendon McCullum, but with many impressive performances by batsmen and bowlers alike, they were one of the most popular teams.

After setting the tone by making 331 for six in their win against Sri Lanka, they struggled to overcome Scotland in a low-scoring encounter after requiring just 143. There were no such difficulties against England, the main drama being their opponent's collapse from 104 for three to 123 all out and New Zealand reaching their target in just 12.2 overs, Finn conceding 49 runs in two overs. For a while, McCullum's onslaught set the possibility of his scoring a century before the target was reached but his dismissal for 77 in just 25 balls ended those hopes. For New Zealand, Tim Southee recorded his country's best-ever World Cup figures with seven for 33. New Zealand would also benefit from Trent Boult's fine bowling which included five for 27 in the win over Australia. A six-wicket win over Afghanistan was followed by their sixth win on the trot after a successful chase of 289 against Bangladesh, opener Martin Guptill registering his side's first century of the tournament.

England would suffer a further poor tournament. It had started far from ideally with Alastair Cook being replaced as captain by Eoin Morgan shortly before the tournament began and after the hefty defeat in front of 84,000 spectators at Melbourne against Australia, they suffered the indignity of losing to New Zealand at Wellington with 37.4 overs remaining. Moeen Ali's century and England's record opening stand of 172 with Ian Bell saw the three-time finalists on their way against Scotland and they indeed batted better against Sri Lanka with a Joe Root century taking them to 309 for six at Wellington. However, centuries from Lahiru Thirimanne and Kumar Sangakkara and partnerships of 100 and 212 saw their opponents very comfortably knock off the runs.

Their denouement at the earliest stage of the competition came against Bangladesh at Adelaide. Impending doom beckoned if they failed to reach the 276 target and when James Anderson was bowled by Rubel Hossain with England fifteen short, their nadir for another World Cup was complete. A rain-reduced win against Afghanistan did little to make the long flight home any more palatable.

Sri Lanka qualified in third place in the same pool courtesy of some fine batting performances. Four batsmen scored centuries in this initial stage whilst Kumar Sangakkara scored a record four centuries in the tournament, all successively. After a heavy defeat to New Zealand, they suffered a further wobble against Afghanistan who had batted spiritedly to score 232. A reply which saw them 18 for three and 51 for four was salvaged by Mahela Jayawardene's 100 which ultimately secured victory by four wickets.

Sangakkara hit his straps in his record tournament with his purple patch starting with an unbeaten 105 against Bangladesh at Melbourne. The main batting honours, though, belonged to Dilshan whose unbeaten 161 saw his side to 332 for one and a comfortable win. For the first of two consecutive games, Sri Lanka started with a century partnership before a second-wicket stand of more than 200. England were brushed aside in this manner at Wellington with Thirimanne joining Sangakkara as the other centurion in the innings.

Despite their defeat in the World Cup's highest match aggregate with Australia, Sangakkara added his third consecutive hundred and the fourth was achieved in their easy win over Scotland at Hobart. Eight centuries were scored and seven century partnerships featured in their impressive top-order batting.

Bangladesh, in their fifth World Cup, qualified for the knock-out stage for the first time taking the final slot in Pool A. A 105-run win against Afghanistan was followed by a 92-run defeat to Sri Lanka but they put in an excellent batting show against Scotland to score 322 in the second innings after conceding 318 to the Associate nation who would have entertained hopes of their first World Cup victory. Tamim Iqbal's 95 was their highest score which included for the first time in their World Cup history four batsmen passing 50.

Their first century was also scored. Mahmudullah's 103 (and wicket-keeper Mushfiqur Rahim's 89) saw off England and although he would add his and his country's second century in the next match against New Zealand, it did not save his side from a three-wicket defeat after setting a creditable 288.

Much credit must be given to Afghanistan in times of turmoil within their country, to even play cricket. To make the World Cup was a fantastic achievement and although they had mixed fortunes, they played an integral part in the pool stage. They bowled out Bangladesh but could only manage 162 in return. A further spirited display with both bat and ball saw them almost notch up a win over Sri Lanka. They were humbled against Australia at Perth conceding the record World Cup total of 417 for six and consigned to a record 275-run defeat and an unsatisfactory match, interrupted by rain, saw them lose to England.

They did, though, record their first victory over Scotland in one of the matches of the tournament. When the first eight Scottish wickets were taken for 144, their chances were high. A ninth-wicket stand of 62 took Scotland to 210 whereupon the Afghan batsmen collapsed to 97 for seven. Undimmed, Samiullah Shenwari found very useful lower-order support and after reaching 96 with five sixes, attempted to reach Afghanistan's first century in the grand manner but failed and 19 runs were required from 19 balls by the last pair. Amidst much tension and a missed run-out opportunity, number 11 Shapoor Zadran saw his side to a famous victory in just their third World Cup match.

The wait for Scotland's first victory thus again went begging. They put in several decent performances but their unwanted record of winless tournaments extending back to 1999 and in their third tournament, continued. They could only manage 142 against the side which went through the pool stage unbeaten, New Zealand, yet only lost by three wickets. The topsy-turvy Afghanistan game offered realistic hope but they fell just short. They lost heavily to England and Sri Lanka but must have felt that the moment had arrived after setting Bangladesh 319 to win in Nelson the game after the Afghanistan match. Kyle Coetzer managed Scotland's first-ever and so far only World Cup century but, after the competition's second-highest successful chase had seen Bangladesh win comparatively easily, his only consolation was that his 156 is the World Cup's highest score in a losing side. Additionally, Matt Machan, captain Preston Mommsen and Richie Berrington all made contributions with the bat as did Josh Davey with the ball.

Pool B saw defending champions, India, make a successful start with their sixth consecutive World Cup win over Pakistan courtesy of a Kohli century. They passed 300 in the next match too against South Africa, registering their first World Cup win in four matches against their opponents with Shikhar Dhawan taking the plaudits with 137. United Arab Emirates did not delay their opponents, but West Indies did make a better fist despite only scoring 182. Captain Jason Holder's 57 at number nine led a recovery but it was his opposing captain, M.S. Dhoni, whose unbeaten 45 gave India their fourth successive win.

Ireland were seen off by eight wickets at Hamilton with Dhawan registering his second century of the tournament. The clean sweep was achieved with a six-wicket victory over Zimbabwe at Auckland but relied upon a Suresh Raina century and an undefeated 85 from Dhoni to see them to their victory target of 288 after recovering from 92 for four.

After their further loss to India, Pakistan then batted abjectly against West Indies finding themselves one for four in a vain search of 311. Fifties from Sohaib Maqsood and Umar Akmal limited the defeat to 150 runs. Although they managed only 235 against Zimbabwe, giant fast bowler, Mohammad Irfan, and Wahab Riaz took four wickets each to see their side to their first win. The second was achieved with an easy 129-run win over United Arab Emirates and they did well to defend 231 – a total bolstered by Duckworth-Lewis after their eventual dismissal for 222 – to beat South Africa at Auckland. A win over Ireland avenged their 2007 defeat and saw them take third place in the pool.

An unbeaten and record fifth-wicket stand of 256 between J-P. Duminy and David Miller set the scene for some rollicking batting by South Africa in the tournament. This stand took them to 339 for four and a 62-run win over Zimbabwe at Hamilton despite a plucky response by the Zimbabwean batsmen. After their first World Cup loss to India (and a total of just 177), just over 23,500 spectators at Sydney's famous ground witnessed an innings of immense butchery from South African captain, A.B. de Villiers. His unbeaten 162 came in 102 minutes and lasted just 66 balls and saw his side to the second total of 400 in World Cup history in a crushing 257-run win.

Remarkably, they managed to beat their 408 for five against West Indies to end on 411 for four against Ireland and a further victory of more than 200 runs. Centuries, although more sedate than de Villiers's effort against West Indies, by Hashim Amla and Faf du Plessis set up the enormous total which was bolstered further by whirlwind cameos by Miller, de Villiers and Rilee Rossouw. It may have come as some surprise that they could not chase 232 against Pakistan but normal service was resumed against United Arab Emirates where de Villiers became the third batsman in the World Cup to be dismissed for 99.

In their return to the World Cup for the first time since 1996, United Arab Emirates performed creditably and were led by the oldest-ever captain in World Cup history, Mohammad Tauqir, who bowed out of the tournament at the age of 43 years and 60 days. He took over the reins from Emirates Airline flight purser, Khurram Khan, at a slightly younger age than his predecessor's 43 years and 164 days on his last captaincy appearance. Khan, before the tournament, became the oldest player to score an ODI century and would have his moments during the competition.

Other players who did well in the tournament included Shaiman Anwar who, against Ireland, scored the first-ever century for the Emirati side and ended with 311 runs in the tournament, the most by any Associate nation player. Fast bowler Amjad Javed also shared in two century partnerships and made 170 runs batting lower down.

Twice, they almost sprung surprises narrowly failing to defend 286 against Zimbabwe and 279 in their next match against Ireland. Perth proved to be an unhappy ground for the Associates, Afghanistan yielding 417 to Australia and the Emirati team managing just 102 against India but, despite not winning a match, they had produced some decent performances.

West Indies arrived in Australasia having four months earlier stopped their Indian tour and gone home without completing it over a contracts dispute with their board. Their only further ODI exposure since the walk-out in October 2014 had been a five-match series in South Africa which they had lost 4-1, the one win coming with the last-wicket pair garnering the necessary 24 runs.

They faced Ireland first in Nelson where Lendl Simmons and Darren Sammy dug them out of a hole with a sixth-wicket stand of 154 and set 305. Ireland, who had chased 328 in the 2011 tournament, comfortably made the runs with more than four overs remaining. Many batting contributions led to a similar total against Pakistan and, after a parlous start to their innings, Pakistan were easily overcome at Christchurch's Hagley Oval.

Against Zimbabwe at Canberra, West Indian captain Jason Holder won the toss and elected to bat first only to see Dwayne Smith dismissed from the second ball of the match. The next wicket fell from the last ball of the innings. In between, carnage ensued as Chris Gayle became the first batsman to hit a World Cup double century and his 16 sixes is the joint-most in an ODI innings. With Marlon Samuels finishing on 133, their stand of 372 is the highest for any wicket in ODI history. Despite a spirited batting performance from Zimbabwe, West Indies' second victory of the tournament came by 73 runs.

What one team can do, another can do better as West Indies came down to earth with a 257-run hiding against South Africa at Sydney.

After conceding the record highest total between two Test playing nations in the World Cup of 408 for five, West Indies collapsed to 151, a total bolstered only by Holder's 56 at number nine. His batting may have slightly made up for becoming the third bowler in World Cup history to go for over 100 runs. A further fifty for Holder against India could not stave off another defeat at Perth but qualification for the knock-out stage was achieved with victory over United Arab Emirates. Jerome Taylor's 14 wickets in the pool stage helped to secure their position.

After their sterling performances in previous tournaments, Ireland seemed the most likely to go deeper into the tournament but, despite three victories, they did not quite manage to do so, their net run rate being inferior to West Indies with whom they ended on the same number of points. Their impressive victory chasing 305 against West Indies rekindled memories of their higher successful chase against England in Bangalore in 2011. This latter victory was achieved through fifties from Paul Stirling, Ed Joyce and Niall O'Brien.

They squeaked through against United Arab Emirates at Brisbane by just two wickets and with only four balls remaining. With five of their bowlers giving away six or more runs an over throughout the competition, they either faced a daunting total or were overwhelmed comparatively easily when bowling second and this was evidenced against South Africa who made 411 for four and won by 201 runs.

They added Zimbabwe to their impressive list of victories in a close match at Hobart where they held on by just five runs after scoring 331 for eight, their highest World Cup total. Ed Joyce became Ireland's fourth World Cup centurion, but Alex Cusack's four wickets saved the day for Ireland after Brendan Taylor and Sean Williams had threatened to spoil the party. Insufficient runs against India and Pakistan – despite captain William Porterfield's 107 – meant that West Indies and not Ireland qualified.

Zimbabwe, re-engaged on the Test scene after the 2011 World Cup, could count a tight win over United Arab Emirates as their solitary victory. Their standout hero was their wicket-keeper and sometimes captain, Brendan Taylor, whose 433 runs in the tournament is a Zimbabwean World Cup record. With a lowest score of 37, Taylor rounded off with centuries against Ireland and India but on both occasions, he ended on the losing side. Three times, Zimbabwe conceded more than 325 including the ignominy of conceding the record ODI partnership of 372 to West Indies.

Sean Williams also had a fine series with 339 runs at an average not far short of Taylor's but there were few bowling successes. They had an opportunity to record the World Cup's highest successful chase against Ireland but fell just five runs short and they restricted Pakistan to just 235 in their 50 overs but the express-paced Pakistani bowlers ultimately defended the total. Four batsmen made starts but Taylor's 50 was the highest score and not quite enough to force their first World Cup victory over a Test-playing country since they beat South Africa in 1999.

Thus were fourteen teams pared down to eight with seven of the forty-nine matches remaining to find the winner. All matches were played under lights but not much electricity was needed at Sydney where Sri Lanka folded tamely for 133 to South Africa. After their impressive pool stage batting, only the very much in-form Sangakkara (45) and Thirimanne (41), batting further down the order, resisted and South Africa cantered home with 32 overs remaining. It was not the result befitting the ODI retirements of Sangakkara and Mahela Jayawardene. Spinners Imran Tahir and Duminy shared seven wickets (including a hit-trick for Duminy) and Quinton de Kock's aggressive, unbeaten 78 saw South Africa again into the semi-finals.

Through Rohit Sharma's 137, India brushed aside the challenge of Bangladesh by 109 runs at Melbourne. In need of 302, no Bangladeshi batsman could pass 35 as they fell well short at 193.

Pakistan took on Australia at Adelaide. Eight Pakistani batsmen reached double figures but Haris Sohail's 41 was top score in their 213. Indeed, this total was the fourth time the same number had been scored in a World Cup knock-out stage, Australia and South Africa both managing it during their epic 1999 semi-final. In 2015, Australia comfortably passed it despite ferocious bowling from Wahab Riaz and a verbal assault on Shane Watson. It brought Riaz two for 54 in nine overs and a fine of 50 per cent of his match fee.

New Zealand took on West Indies at Wellington where a non-verbal but brutal batting blitz by Martin Guptill not only trumped Gayle's double hundred the previous month to make the New Zealand opener the World Cup's highest scorer but took his side to the semi-finals for the seventh time. Of Guptill's unbeaten 237, 162 were scored in boundaries and took New Zealand to 393 for six. His innings was only 13 fewer than West Indies managed in reply despite their hitting more sixes than New Zealand.

Fate decreed that the competition's perennial bridesmaids of South Africa and New Zealand with four and seven World Cup semi-final appearances without a final should be brought together and for one to finally reach a final. It was South Africa who in general held sway but an inopportune rain break restricted them to a final total of 281 for five in 43 overs with New Zealand's target fixed at 298 in the same number of overs.

Like South Africa's innings, there were several contributions from New Zealand's batsmen but errors in the field meant that the home team reached the final over requiring 12. After two balls, pace bowler Steyn needed treatment for cramp but, with the fifth ball of the over, it was South Africa-born Grant Elliott, playing for New Zealand, whose six sparked celebrations for the home team and further despair for South Africa. Elliott's unbeaten 84 won him the Man of the Match award.

Australia against India at Sydney, a repeat of the 2003 Johannesburg final, was less dramatic and ended with the same team victorious, this time by 95 runs. Australia's 328 for seven was built around a second-wicket partnership of 182 between Finch and Steve Smith, the latter continuing his fine form against India. Although four batsmen made good starts, India was always behind the rate and not even one of the finest finishers, Dhoni, with a run-a-ball 65 could take his team to the final and a chance to defend their trophy.

Like 2011, the co-hosts contested the eleventh World Cup final in front of 93,000 spectators at Melbourne. It was a game where ball predominantly dominated bat but when Brendon McCullum was bowled in the first over by the impressive Starc, any advantage of winning the toss was quickly negated. Further wickets fell and, in a strange comparison with the 1979 final, a low total included a century partnership and a high number of ducks. New Zealand were indebted to a 111-run, fourth- wicket stand between Ross Taylor and the semi-final award winner, Elliott, but could only reach 183 after appearing to have weathered the storm.

Although an early inroad was made with Boult's quick dismissal of Finch, captain Michael Clarke, playing in his last ODI innings, made 74 and, with Smith's slightly less restrained 56, victory was achieved by seven wickets with almost 17 overs unused as Australia recorded their fifth World Cup victory.

2015 MISCELLANY

- The highest World Cup total without a century was achieved with South Africa's 341 for six against United Arab Emirates at Wellington.
- The 2015 competition saw two of only five World Cup occasions of two bowlers on opposing sides taking five wickets each in the same match. Steven Finn and Mitchell Marsh did so in the England and Australia match at Melbourne as did Trent Boult and Mitchell Starc in the New Zealand and Australia match at Auckland.
- For the first time since 1987, no side was dismissed for under 100.
- The lowest World Cup total without a duck was achieved by United Arab Emirates with 102 in their match against India at Perth.
- Although Mitchell Starc played in all of Australia's eight matches, he did not make a run in the tournament in his three innings.
- With seven appearances, Australia have more than double the number of World Cup final appearances than any other nation. West Indies, India, Sri Lanka and England have all reached three.
- Scotland's Josh Davey's fifteen wickets in the competition is the most in any World Cup tournament by an Associate nation player.

2015 STATISTICS

HIGHEST TOTALS	
417 for 6 in 50 overs	Australia vs. Afghanistan at Perth
411 for 4 in 50 overs	South Africa vs. Ireland at Canberra
408 for 5 in 50 overs	South Africa vs. West Indies at Sydney
393 for 6 in 50 overs	New Zealand vs. West Indies at Wellington

LOWEST COMPLETED TOTALS	
102 in 31.3 overs	United Arab Emirates vs. India at Perth
123 in 33.2 overs	England vs. New Zealand at Wellington
130 in 25.4 overs	Scotland vs. Australia at Hobart
133 in 37.2 overs	Sri Lanka vs. South Africa at Sydney

HIGHEST MATCH AGGREGATES	
688 for 18 wickets	Australia (376-9) vs. Sri Lanka (312-9) at Sydney
661 for 12 wickets	West Indies (372-2) vs. Zimbabwe (289) at Canberra
657 for 18 wickets	Ireland (331-8) vs. Zimbabwe (326) at Hobart

HIGHEST MATCH AGGREGATES

643 for 16 wickets	New Zealand (393-6) vs. West Indies (250) at Wellington
640 for 12 wickets	Scotland (318-8) vs. Bangladesh (322-4) at Nelson

LOWEST MATCH AGGREGATES WITH RESULT

206 for 11 wickets	United Arab Emirates (102) vs. India (104-1) at Perth
212 for 8 wickets	Afghanistan (111-7) vs. England (101-1) at Sydney
248 for 12 wickets	England (123) vs. New Zealand (125-2) at Wellington

BIGGEST VICTORY MARGINS

275 runs	Australia (417-6) vs. Afghanistan (142) at Perth
257 runs	South Africa (408-5) vs. West Indies (151) at Sydney
201 runs	South Africa (411-4) vs. Ireland (210) at Canberra
9 wickets	India (104-1) vs. United Arab Emirates (102) at Perth
9 wickets	Sri Lanka (312-1) vs. England (309-6) at Wellington
9 wickets	England (101-1) vs. Afghanistan (111-7) at Sydney
9 wickets	South Africa (134-1) vs. Sri Lanka (133) at Sydney

LOWEST VICTORY MARGINS

5 runs	Ireland (331-8) vs. Zimbabwe (326) at Hobart
15 runs	Bangladesh (275-7) vs. England (260) at Adelaide
1 wicket	Afghanistan (211-9) vs. Scotland (210) at Dunedin
1 wicket	New Zealand (152-9) vs. Australia (151) at Auckland

LEADING RUN SCORERS

547 (average 68.38)	Martin Guptill (New Zealand)
541 (average 108.20)	Kumar Sangakkara (Sri Lanka)
482 (average 96.40)	Abraham de Villiers (South Africa)

HIGHEST SCORERS

237*	Martin Guptill	New Zealand vs. West Indies at Wellington
215	Chris Gayle	West Indies vs. Zimbabwe at Canberra
178	David Warner	Australia vs. Afghanistan at Perth
162*	Abraham de Villiers	South Africa vs. West Indies at Sydney
161*	Tillakaratne Dilshan	Sri Lanka vs. Bangladesh at Melbourne

CENTURIES
Thirty-eight

LEADING WICKET TAKERS	
22 (average 10.18)	Mitchell Starc (Australia)
22 (average 16.86)	Trent Boult (New Zealand)
18 (average 17.83)	Umesh Yadav (India)

BEST BOWLING PERFORMANCES		
9-0-33-7	Tim Southee	New Zealand vs. England at Wellington
9-0-28-6	Mitchell Starc	Australia vs. New Zealand at Auckland
10-3-27-5	Trent Boult	New Zealand vs. Australia at Auckland
9-0-33-5	Mitchell Marsh	Australia vs. England at Melbourne

FIVE WICKETS IN AN INNINGS
Seven

HIGHEST PARTNERSHIPS FOR EACH WICKET				
1	174	Rohit Sharma & Shikhar Dhawan	Ind. vs. Ire.	Hamilton
2	372	Chris Gayle & Marlon Samuels	WI vs. Zim.	Canberra
3	143	Martin Guptill & Ross Taylor	NZ vs. WI	Wellington
4	146	Aaron Finch & George Bailey	Aus. vs. Eng.	Melbourne
5	256*	David Miller & Jean-Paul Duminy	SA vs. Zim.	Hamilton
6	154	Lendl Simmons & Darren Sammy	WI vs. Ire.	Nelson
7	107	Amjad Javed & Nasir Aziz	UAE vs. WI	Napier
7	107	Shaiman Anwar & Amjad Javed	UAE vs. Ire.	Brisbane
8	53*	Amjad Javed & Mohammad Naveed	UAE vs. Zim.	Nelson
9	62	Majid Haq & Alasdair Evans	Sco. vs. Afg.	Dunedin
10	45	Brad Haddin & Pat Cummins	Aus. vs. NZ	Auckland

WORLD CUP
COUNTRY RECORDS

AFGHANISTAN

Highest total	232 in 49.4 overs vs. Sri Lanka at Dunedin in 2015
Lowest completed total	142 in 37.3 overs vs. Australia at Perth in 2015
Highest match aggregate	559 for 16 wickets with Australia at Perth in 2015
Lowest match aggregate with result	212 for 8 wickets with England at Sydney in 2015
Biggest victory margin	1 wicket vs. Scotland at Dunedin in 2015
Biggest defeats	275 runs vs. Australia at Perth in 2015
	9 wickets vs. England at Sydney
Highest score	96 Samiullah Shenwari vs. Scotland at Dunedin in 2015
Most career runs	254 (average 42.33) Samiullah Shenwari
Centuries for	0
Centuries against	2
Best bowling	4-38 Shapoor Zadran vs. Scotland at Dunedin in 2015
Most career wickets	10 (average 26.50) Shapoor Zadran
Five wickets in an innings for	0
Five wickets in an innings against	0

Highest partnership for each wicket		
1	42	Javed Ahmadi & Nawroz Mangal vs. Scotland at Dunedin in 2015
2	6	Javed Ahmadi & Asghar Stanikzai vs. Sri Lanka at Dunedin in 2015
3	88	Asghar Stanikzai & Samiullah Shenwari vs. Sri Lanka at Dunedin in 2015
4	62	Nawroz Mangal & Samiullah Shenwari vs. Bangladesh at Canberra in 2015
5	31	Nasir Ahmadzai & Shafiqullah Shinwari vs. England at Sydney in 2015
6	58	Mohammad Nabi & Najibullah Zadran vs. Bangladesh at Canberra in 2015
7	86	Samiullah Shenwari & Najibullah Zadran vs. New Zealand at Napier in 2015
8	35	Samiullah Shenwari & Dawlat Zadran vs. Scotland at Dunedin in 2015
9	60	Samiullah Shenwari & Hamid Hassan vs. Scotland at Dunedin in 2015
10	20	Hamid Hassan & Shapoor Zadran vs. New Zealand at Napier in 2015

Position in each World Cup	
1975	No appearance
1979	No appearance
1983	No appearance
1987	No appearance
1992	No appearance
1996	No appearance
1999	No appearance
2003	No appearance
2007	No appearance
2011	No appearance
2015	Group stage

AUSTRALIA

Highest total	417 for 6 in 50 overs vs. Afghanistan at Perth in 2015
Lowest completed total	129 in 38.2 overs vs. India at Chelmsford in 1983

Highest match aggregate	688 for 18 wickets with Sri Lanka at Sydney in 2015
Lowest match aggregate with result	183 for 11 wickets with Ireland at Bridgetown in 2007
Biggest victory margins	275 runs vs. Afghanistan at Perth in 2015
	10 wickets vs. Bangladesh at North Sound in 2007
Biggest defeats	118 runs vs. India at Chelmsford in 1983
	9 wickets vs. South Africa at Sydney in 1992
Highest score	178 David Warner vs. Afghanistan at Perth in 2015
Most career runs	1743 (average 45.87) Ricky Ponting
Centuries for	26
Centuries against	9
Best bowling	7 for 15 Glenn McGrath vs. Namibia at Potchefstroom, in 2003
Most career wickets	71 (average 18.20) Glenn McGrath
Five wickets in an innings for	13
Five wickets in an innings against	6

Highest partnership for each wicket		
1	183	Shane Watson & Brad Haddin vs. Canada at Bangalore in 2011
2	260	David Warner & Steve Smith vs. Afghanistan at Perth in 2015
3	234*	Ricky Ponting & Damien Martyn vs India at Johannesburg in 2003
4	204	Michael Clarke & Brad Hodge vs. Netherlands at Basseterre in 2007
5	160	Glenn Maxwell & Shane Watson vs. Sri Lanka at Sydney in 2015
6	99	Ross Edwards & Rod Marsh vs. West Indies at The Oval in 1975
7	70*	Darren Lehmann & Brad Hogg vs. Namibia at Potchefstoom in 2003
8	97	Michael Bevan & Andy Bichel vs. New Zealand at Port Elizabeth in 2003
9	73*	Michael Bevan & Andy Bichel vs. England at Port Elizabeth in 2003
10	45	Brad Haddin & Pat Cummins vs. New Zealand at Auckland in 2015

Position in each World Cup	
1975	Runner-up
1979	Group stage
1983	Group stage
1987	Winner
1992	Group stage
1996	Runner-up
1999	Winner
2003	Winner
2007	Winner
2011	Quarter-final
2015	Winner

BANGLADESH

Highest total	322 for 4 in 48.1 overs vs. Scotland at Nelson in 2015
Lowest completed total	58 in 18.5 overs vs. West Indies at Dhaka in 2011
Highest match aggregate	653 for 13 wickets with India at Dhaka in 2011
Lowest match aggregate with result	117 for 11 wickets with West Indies at Dhaka in 2011
Biggest victory margins	105 runs vs. Afghanistan at Canberra in 2015
	7 wickets vs. Bermuda at Port of Spain in 2007
Biggest defeats	206 runs vs. South Africa at Dhaka in 2011
	10 wickets (on three occasions) vs. Sri Lanka at Pietermaritzburg in 2003; vs. South Africa at Bloemfontein in 2003 and vs. Australia at North Sound in 2007
Highest score	128* Mahmudullah vs. New Zealand at Hamilton in 2015
Most career runs	540 (average 30.00) Shakib Al Hasan
Centuries for	2
Centuries against	9

Best bowling	4 for 21 Shafiul Islam vs. Ireland at Dhaka in 2011
Most career wickets	23 (average 35.78) Shakib Al Hasan
Five wickets in an innings for	0
Five wickets in an innings against	4

Highest partnership for each wicket		
1	69	Shahriar Hossain & Mehrab Hossain vs.Pakistan at Northampton in 1999
2	139	Tamim Iqbal & Mahmudullah vs. Scotland at Nelson in 2015
3	90	Soumya Sarkar & Mahmudullah vs. New Zealand at Hamilton in 2015
4	84	Mushfiqur Rahim & Shakib Al Hasan vs. India at Port of Spain in 2007
5	141	Mahmudullah & Mushfiqur Rahim vs. England at Adelaide in 2015
6	78	Mahmudullah & Sabbir Rahman vs. New Zealand at Hamilton in 2015
7	58	Mushfiqur Rahim & Mashrafe Mortaza vs West Indies at Bridgetown in 2007
8	70*	Khaled Mashud & Mohammad Rafique vs. New Zealand at Kimberley in 2003
9	58*	Mahmudullah & Shafiul Islam vs. England at Chittagong in 2011
10	34	Mohammad Rafique & Syed Rasal vs.New Zealand at North Sound in 2007

Position in each World Cup	
1975	No appearance
1979	No appearance
1983	No appearance
1987	No appearance
1992	No appearance
1996	No appearance
1999	Group stage
2003	Group stage
2007	Super 8 stage
2011	Group stage
2015	Quarter-final

ENGLAND

Highest total	338 for 8 in 50 overs vs. India at Bangalore in 2011
Lowest completed total	93 in 36.2 overs vs. Australia at Leeds in 1975
Highest match aggregate	676 for 18 wickets with India at Bangalore in 2011
Lowest match aggregate with result	91 for 12 wickets with Canada at Manchester in 1979
Biggest victory margins	202 runs vs. India at Lord's in 1975
	9 wickets (on three occasions) vs. Sri Lanka at Leeds in 1983; vs. Kenya at Canterbury in 1999 and vs. Afghanistan at Sydney in 2015
Biggest defeats	122 runs vs. South Africa at The Oval in 1999
	10 wickets vs. Sri Lanka at Colombo in 2011
Highest score	158 Andrew Strauss vs. India at Bangalore in 2011
Most career runs	897 (average 44.85) Graham Gooch
Centuries for	11
Centuries against	12
Best bowling	5 for 39 Vic Marks vs. Sri Lanka at Taunton in 1983
Most career wickets	30 (average 25.40) Ian Botham
Five wickets in an innings for	3
Five wickets in an innings against	8

Highest partnership for each wicket		
1	172	Moeen Ali & Ian Bell vs. Scotland at Christchurch in 2015
2	176	Dennis Amiss & Keith Fletcher vs. India at Lord's in 1975
3	170	Andrew Strauss & Ian Bell vs. India at Bangalore in 2011
4	115	Allan Lamb & Mike Gatting vs. New Zealand at The Oval in 1983
5	98	Joe Root & James Taylor vs. Sri Lanka at Wellington in 2015
6	98	David Gower & Ian Gould vs. Sri Lanka at Taunton in 1983
7	92	James Taylor & Chris Woakes vs. Australia at Melbourne in 2015

Highest partnership for each wicket		
8	71*	Paul Nixon & Liam Plunkett vs. New Zealand at Gros Islet in 2007
9	55	Andrew Flintoff & Andrew Caddick vs. India at Durban in 2003
10	36	James Taylor & James Anderson vs. Australia at Melbourne in 2015

Position in each World Cup	
1975	Semi-final
1979	Runner-up
1983	Semi-final
1987	Runner-up
1992	Runner-up
1996	Quarter-final
1999	Group stage
2003	Group stage
2007	Super 8 stage
2011	Quarter-final
2015	Group stage

INDIA

Highest total	413 for 5 in 50 overs vs. Bermuda at Port of Spain in 2007
Lowest completed total	125 in 41.4 overs vs. Australia at Centurion in 2003
Highest match aggregate	676 for 18 wickets with England at Bangalore in 2011
Lowest match aggregate with result	206 for 11 wickets with United Arab Emirates at Perth in 2015
Biggest victory margins	257 runs vs. Bermuda at Port of Spain in 2007
	10 wickets vs. East Africa at Leeds in 1975
Biggest defeats	202 runs vs. England at Lord's in 1975
	9 wickets (twice) vs. West Indies at Birmingham in 1979 and vs. Australia at Centurion in 2003
Highest score	183 Sourav Ganguly vs. Sri Lanka at Taunton in 1999

Most career runs	2278 (average 56.95) Sachin Tendulkar
Centuries for	25
Centuries against	15
Best bowling	6 for 23 Ashish Nehra vs. England at Durban in 2003
Most career wickets	44 (average 20.23) Zaheer Khan and Javagal Srinath (average 27.82)
Five wickets in an innings for	5
Five wickets in an innings against	7

Highest partnership for each wicket		
1	174	Rohit Sharma & Shikhar Dhawan vs. Ireland at Hamilton in 2015
2	318	Sourav Ganguly & Rahul Dravid vs. Sri Lanka at Taunton in 1999
3	237*	Sachin Tendulkar & Rahul Dravid vs. Kenya at Bristol in 1999
4	142	Navjot Sidhu & Vinod Kambli vs. Zimbabwe at Kanpur in 1996
5	196*	Suresh Raina & Mahendra Singh Dhoni vs Zimbabwe at Auckland in 2015
6	74*	Yuvraj Singh & Suresh Raina vs. Australia at Ahmedabad in 2011
7	58	Kapil Dev & Madan Lal vs. Australia at Nottingham in 1983
8	82*	Kapil Dev & Kiran More vs. New Zealand at Bangalore in 1987
9	126*	Kapil Dev & Syed Kirmani vs. Zimbabwe at Tunbridge Wells in 1983
10	32	Zaheer Khan & Munaf Patel vs. Bangladesh at Port of Spain in 2007

Position in each World Cup	
1975	Group stage
1979	Group stage
1983	Winner
1987	Semi-final
1992	Group stage
1996	Semi-final
1999	Super 6 stage

2003	Runner-up
2007	Group stage
2011	Winner
2015	Semi-final

NEW ZEALAND

Highest total	393 for 6 in 50 overs vs. West Indies at Wellington in 2015
Lowest completed total	112 in 30.1 overs vs. Australia at Port Elizabeth in 2003
Highest match aggregate	643 for 16 wickets with West Indies at Wellington in 2015
Lowest match aggregate with result	141 for 10 wickets with Kenya at Chennai in 2011
Biggest victory margins	181 runs vs. East Africa at Birmingham in 1975
	10 wickets (twice) vs. Kenya at Chennai in 2011 and vs. Zimbabwe at Ahmedabad in 2011
Biggest defeats	215 runs vs. Australia at St. George's in 2007
	9 wickets (twice) vs.India at Nagpur in 1987 and vs. Pakistan at Manchester in 1999
Highest score	237* Martin Guptill vs. West Indies at Wellington in 2015
Most career runs	1075 (average 35.83) Stephen Fleming
Centuries for	15
Centuries against	16
Best bowling	7 for 33 Tim Southee vs. England at Wellington in 2015
Most career wickets	36 (average 21.33) Jacob Oram and Daniel Vettori (average 32.44)
Five wickets in an innings for	4
Five wickets in an innings against	3

		Highest partnership for each wicket
1	166*	Martin Guptill & Brendon McCullum vs. Zimbabwe at Ahmedabad in 2011
2	140*	Stephen Fleming & Nathan Astle vs. South Africa at Johannesburg in 2003
3	149	Glenn Turner & John Parker vs. East Africa at Birmingham in 1975
4	168	Lee Germon & Chris Harris vs. Australia at Chennai in 1996
5	148	Roger Twose & Chris Cairns vs. Australia at Cardiff in 1999
6	85*	Jacob Oram & Brendon McCullum vs. Canada at Gros Islet in 2007
7	85	Ross Taylor & Jacob Oram vs. Pakistan at Pallekele in 2011
8	71	Brendon McCullum & James Franklin vs. Ireland at Providence in 2007
9	59	Jeremy Coney & John Bracewell vs. Pakistan at Nottingham in 1983
10	65	Martin Snedden & Ewen Chatfield vs. Sri Lanka at Derby in 1983

Position in each World Cup	
1975	Semi-final
1979	Semi-final
1983	Group stage
1987	Group stage
1992	Semi-final
1996	Quarter-final
1999	Semi-final
2003	Super 6 stage
2007	Semi-final
2011	Semi-final
2015	Runner-up

PAKISTAN

Highest total	349 in 49.5 overs vs. Zimbabwe at Kingston in 2007
Lowest completed total	74 in 40.2 overs vs. England at Adelaide in 1992

Highest match aggregate	626 for 14 wickets with Sri Lanka at Swansea in 1983
Lowest match aggregate with result	221 for 10 wickets with United Arab Emirates at Gujranwala in 1996
Biggest victory margins	205 runs vs. Kenya at Hambantota in 2011
	10 wickets vs. West Indies at Dhaka in 2011
Biggest defeats	150 runs vs. West Indies at Christchurch in 2015
	10 wickets vs. West Indies at Melbourne in 1992
Highest score	160 Imran Nazir vs. Zimbabwe at Kingston in 2007
Most career runs	1083 (average 43.32) Javed Miandad
Centuries for	14
Centuries against	5
Best bowling	5 for 16 Shahid Afridi vs. Kenya at Hambantota in 2011
Most career wickets	55 (average 23.84) Wasim Akram
Five wickets in an innings for	7
Five wickets in an innings against	4

Highest partnership for each wicket		
1	194	Saeed Anwar & Wajahatullah Wasti vs. New Zealand at Manchester in 1999
2	167	Ramiz Raja & Salim Malik vs. England at Karachi in 1987
3	145	Aamer Sohail & Javed Miandad vs. Zimbabwe at Hobart in 1992
4	147*	Zaheer Abbas & Imran Khan vs. New Zealand at Nottingham in 1983
5	118	Misbah-ul-Haq & Umar Akmal vs. Kenya at Hambantota in 2011
6	144	Imran Khan & Shahid Mahboob vs. Sri Lanka at Leeds in 1983
7	74	Azhar Mahmood & Wasim Akram vs. West Indies at Bristol in 1999
8	54	Rashid Latif & Wasim Akram vs. Australia at Johannesburg in 2003
9	66	Abdul Razzaq & Umar Gul vs. New Zealand at Pallekele in 2011
10	54	Saqlain Mushtaq & Shoaib Akhtar vs. England at Cape Town in 2003

Position in each World Cup	
1975	Group stage
1979	Semi-final
1983	Semi-final
1987	Semi-final
1992	Winner
1996	Quarter-final
1999	Runner-up
2003	Group stage
2007	Group stage
2011	Semi-final
2015	Quarter-final

SOUTH AFRICA

Highest total	411 for 4 in 50 overs vs. Ireland at Canberra in 2015
Lowest completed total	149 in 43.5 overs vs. Australia at Gros Islet in 2007
Highest match aggregate	671 for 16 wickets with Australia at Basseterre in 2007
Lowest match aggregate with result	217 for 10 with Bangladesh at Bloemfontein in 2003
Biggest victory margins	257 runs vs. West Indies at Sydney in 2015
	10 wickets (twice) vs. Kenya at Potchefstroom in 2003 and vs. Bangladesh at Bloemfontein in 2003
Biggest defeats	130 runs vs. India at Melbourne in 2015
	9 wickets vs. New Zealand at Johannesburg in 2003
Highest score	188* Gary Kirsten vs. United Arab Emirates at Rawalpindi in 1996
Most career runs	1207 (average 63.53) Abraham de Villiers
Centuries for	14
Centuries against	9

Best bowling	5 for 18 Andrew Hall vs. England at Bridgetown in 2007
Most career wickets	38 (average 24.03) Allan Donald
Five wickets in an innings for	7
Five wickets in an innings against	0

Highest partnership for each wicket		
1	186	Gary Kirsten & Andrew Hudson vs. Netherlands at Rawalpindi in 1996
2	247	Hashim Amla & Faf du Plessis vs. Ireland at Canberra in 2015
3	221	Hashim Amla & Abraham de Villiers vs. Netherlands at Mohali in 2011
4	134*	Jacques Kallis & Mark Boucher vs. Netherlands at Basseterre in 2007
	134	Abraham de Villiers & Rilee Rossouw vs. West Indies at Sydney in 2015
5	256*	David Miller & Jean-Paul Duminy vs. Zimbabwe at Hamilton in 2015
6	87	Jean-Paul Duminy & Colin Ingram vs. Ireland at Kolkata in 2011
7	66	Daryll Cullinan & Shaun Pollock vs. Zimbabwe at Chelmsford in 1999
8	67	Lance Klusener & Nicky Boje vs. West Indies at Cape Town in 2003
9	44	Lance Klusener & Steve Elworthy vs. Sri Lanka at Northampton in 1999
10	35	Lance Klusener & Allan Donald vs. Zimbabwe at Chelmsford in 1999

Position in each World Cup	
1975	No appearance
1979	No appearance
1983	No appearance
1987	No appearance
1992	Semi-final
1996	Quarter-final
1999	Semi-final
2003	Group stage
2007	Semi-final
2011	Quarter-final
2015	Semi-final

SRI LANKA

Highest total	398 for 5 in 50 overs vs. Kenya at Kandy in 1996
Lowest completed total	86 in 37.2 overs vs. West Indies at Manchester in 1975
Highest match aggregate	688 for 18 wickets with Australia at Sydney in 2015
Lowest match aggregate with result	73 for 11 wickets with Canada at Paarl in 2003
Biggest victory margins	243 runs vs. Bermuda at Port of Spain in 2007
	10 wickets (twice) vs. England at Colombo in 2011 and vs. Bangladesh at Pietermaritzburg in 2003
Biggest defeats	192 runs vs. Pakistan at Nottingham in 1975
	9 wickets (on four occasions) vs. West Indies at Manchester in 1975; vs. New Zealand at Nottingham in 1979; vs. England at Leeds in 1983 and vs. South Africa at Sydney in 2015
Highest score	161* Tillakaratne Dilshan vs. Bangladesh at Melbourne in 2015
Most career runs	1532 (average 56.74) Kumar Sangakkara
Centuries for	23
Centuries against	18
Best bowling	6 for 25 Chaminda Vaas vs. Bangladesh at Pietermaritzburg in 2003
Most career wickets	68 (average 19.63) Muttiah Muralitharan
Five wickets in an innings for	4
Five wickets in an innings against	6

Highest partnership for each wicket		
1	282	Upul Tharanga & Tillakaratne Dilshan vs. Zimbabwe at Pallekele in 2011
2	212*	Lahiru Thirimanne & Kumar Sangakkara vs. England at Wellington in 2015
3	183	Asanka Gurusinha & Aravinda de Silva vs. Kenya at Kandy in 1996
	183	Sanath Jayasuriya & Mahela Jayawardene vs. West Indies at Providence in 2007

Highest partnership for each wicket		
4	152	Marvan Atapattu & Aravinda de Silva vs. South Africa at Durban in 2003
5	131*	Arjuna Ranatunga & Hashan Tillakaratne vs. India at Delhi in 1996
6	97	Tillakaratne Dilshan & Russel Arnold vs. South Africa at Providence in 2007
7	58*	Jeevan Mendis & Thisara Perera vs. Afghanistan at Dunedin in 2015
8	64	Mahela Jayawardene & Chaminda Vaas vs. Kenya at Southampton in 1999
9	35	Guy de Alwis & Rumesh Ratnayake vs. England at Taunton in 1983
10	33	Rumesh Ratnayake & Vinothen John vs. England at Leeds in 1983

Position in each World Cup	
1975	Group stage
1979	Group stage
1983	Group stage
1987	Group stage
1992	Group stage
1996	Winner
1999	Group stage
2003	Semi-final
2007	Runner-up
2011	Runner-up
2015	Quarter-final

WEST INDIES

Highest total	372-2 in 50 overs vs. Zimbabwe at Canberra in 2015
Lowest completed total	93 in 35.2 overs vs. Kenya at Pune in 1996
Highest match aggregate	661 for 12 wickets with Zimbabwe at Canberra in 2015
Lowest match aggregate with result	117 for 11 wickets with Bangladesh at Dhaka in 2011
Biggest victory margins	215 runs vs. Netherlands at Delhi in 2011
	10 wickets (twice) vs. Zimbabwe at Birmingham in 1983 and vs. Pakistan at Melbourne in 1992

Biggest defeats	257 runs vs. South Africa at Sydney in 2015
	10 wickets vs. Pakistan at Dhaka in 2011
Highest score	215 Chris Gayle vs. Zimbabwe at Canberra in 2015
Most career runs	1225 (average 42.24) Brian Lara
Centuries for	17
Centuries against	12
Best bowling	7 for 51 Winston Davis vs. Australia at Leeds in 1983
Most career wickets	27 (average 20.26) Courtney Walsh
Five wickets in an innings for	6
Five wickets in an innings against	3

Highest partnership for each wicket		
1	175*	Desmond Haynes & Brian Lara vs. Pakistan at Melbourne in 1992
2	372	Chris Gayle & Marlon Samuels vs. Zimbabwe at Canberra in 2015
3	195*	Gordon Greenidge & Larry Gomes vs. Zimbabwe at Worcester in 1983
4	149	Rohan Kanhai & Clive Lloyd vs. Australia at Lord's in 1975
5	139	Viv Richards & Collis King vs. England at Lord's in 1979
6	154	Lendl Simmons & Darren Sammy vs. Ireland at Nelson in 2015
7	98	Ramnaresh Sarwan & Ridley Jacobs vs. New Zealand at Port Elizabeth in 2003
8	45	Denesh Ramdin & Jason Holder vs. South Africa at Sydney in 2015
9	51	Jason Holder & Jerome Taylor vs. India at Perth in 2015
10	71	Andy Roberts & Joel Garner vs. India at Manchester in 1983

Position in each World Cup	
1975	Winner
1979	Winner
1983	Runner-up

Position in each World Cup	
1987	Group stage
1992	Group stage
1996	Semi-final
1999	Group stage
2003	Group stage
2007	Super 8 stage
2011	Quarter-final
2015	Quarter-final

WORLD CUP GROUND RECORDS

BRISTOL

Gloucestershire's main ground first hosted an ODI during the 1983 World Cup and held two further in 1999. In total, sixteen games have been held there since it became a regular venue in 2000. The Nevil Road ground has also been used for T20 Internationals. The ground can hold 17,500 for international matches.

World Cup matches hosted	3	
Highest total	329-2	India vs. Kenya in 1999
Lowest completed total	202	West Indies vs. Pakistan in 1999
Highest match aggregate	564-9	India (329-2) vs. Kenya (235-7) in 1999
Lowest match aggregate	415-15	Sri Lanka (206) vs. New Zealand (209-5) in 1983
Highest score	140*	Sachin Tendulkar India vs. Kenya in 1999
Centuries	2	Sachin Tendulkar 140* and Rahul Dravid 104* India vs. Kenya in 1999
Best bowling	5-25	Richard Hadlee New Zealand vs. Sri Lanka in 1983
Five wickets in an innings	1	Hadlee (above)
Highest partnership	237*	Sachin Tendulkar & Rahul Dravid India vs. Kenya in 1999 for the third wicket

2019 schedule	
1 June	Afghanistan vs. Australia (d/n)
7 June	Pakistan vs. Sri Lanka
11 June	Bangladesh vs. Sri Lanka

CARDIFF

Glamorgan's home ground held its first ODI during the 1999 World Cup and four further games will be played during the 2019 tournament. The ground has hosted 24 ODIs after becoming a regular in 2001 as well as Tests and T20 Internationals. Around 15,500 can be accommodated during international matches.

World Cup matches hosted	1	
Highest total	214-5	New Zealand vs. Australia in 1999
Lowest completed total	213-8	Australia vs. New Zealand in 1999
Highest match aggregate	427-13	Australia (213-8) vs. New Zealand (214-5) in 1999
Lowest match aggregate	427-13	As above
Highest score	80*	Roger Twose New Zealand vs. Australia in 1999
Centuries	0	
Best bowling	4-37	Geoff Allott New Zealand vs. Australia in 1999
Five wickets in an innings	0	
Highest partnership	148	Roger Twose & Chris Cairns New Zealand vs. Australia in 1999 for the fifth wicket

2019 schedule	
1 June	New Zealand vs. Sri Lanka
4 June	Afghanistan vs. Sri Lanka
8 June	England vs. Bangladesh
15 June	South Africa vs. Afghanistan (d/n)

CHESTER-LE-STREET

Durham's delightful ground, renowned for its setting close to Lumley Castle, first held international fixtures during the 1999 World Cup. A regular venue since 2000 having hosted now sixteen ODIs in addition to Tests and T20 Internationals, three further games will be played during the 2019 World Cup. Ground capacity is 19,000 for international matches.

World Cup matches hosted	2	
Highest total	261-6	Pakistan vs. Scotland in 1999
Lowest completed total	167	Scotland vs. Pakistan in 1999

Highest match aggregate	428-16	Pakistan (261-6) vs. Scotland (167) in 1999
Lowest match aggregate	359-10	Bangladesh (178-7) vs. Australia (181-3) in 1999
Highest score	81*	Yousuf Youhana (now Mohammad Yousuf) Pakistan vs. Scotland in 1999
Centuries	0	
Best bowling	3-11	Shoaib Akhtar Pakistan vs. Scotland in 1999
Five wickets in an innings	0	
Highest partnership	103	Mohammad Yousuf & Moin Khan Pakistan vs. Scotland in 1999 for the sixth wicket

2019 schedule	
28 June	Sri Lanka vs. South Africa
1 July	Sri Lanka vs. West Indies
3 July	England vs. New Zealand

EDGBASTON

Birmingham's ground, home of Warwickshire, was one of the first English grounds used for ODIs and has hosted fifty-eight since 1972. It has featured in all World Cups held in England and has played host to many Tests and also T20 Internationals. It can hold almost 25,000 people. The Australia and South Africa 1999 semi-final World Cup match, one of the most famous, took place at Edgbaston.

World Cup matches hosted	11	
Highest total	309-5	New Zealand vs. East Africa in 1975
Lowest completed total	94	East Africa vs. England in 1975
Highest match aggregate	533-16	Pakistan (266-7) vs. West Indies (267-9) in 1975
Lowest match aggregate	211-13	Canada (105) vs. Australia (106-3) in 1979
Highest score	171*	Glenn Turner New Zealand vs. East Africa in 1975
Centuries	2	Glenn Turner 171* New Zealand vs. East Africa 1975 and 106* Gordon Greenidge West Indies vs. India in 1979

Best bowling	5-21	Alan Hurst Australia vs. Canada in 1979
Five wickets in an innings	2	Alan Hurst 5-21 Australia vs. Canada 1979 and 5-36 Shaun Pollock South Africa vs. Australia in 1999
Highest partnership	176	Gary Kirsten & Herschelle Gibbs South Africa vs. New Zealand in 1999 for the first wicket

2019 schedule	
19 June	New Zealand vs. South Africa
26 June	New Zealand vs. Pakistan
30 June	England vs. India
2 July	Bangladesh vs. India
11 July	Second semi-final 2nd vs. 3rd

HEADINGLEY

A venue which has held ODIs since 1973 and Tests since 1899, Yorkshire's famous Leeds ground will add four further matches during the World Cup to its existing forty. The ground can hold up to 17,500. Headingley has held the most World Cup matches of any ground and many of the memorable moments have taken place there.

World Cup matches hosted	12	
Highest total	278-7	Australia vs. Pakistan in 1975
Lowest completed total	93	England vs. Australia in 1975
Highest match aggregate	543-12	South Africa (271-7) vs. Australia (272-5) in 1999
Lowest match aggregate	187-16	England (93) vs. Australia (94-6) in 1975
Highest score	120*	Steve Waugh Australia vs. South Africa in 1999
Centuries	3	Steve Waugh 120* Australia vs. Pakistan 1999; 102* Imran Khan Pakistan vs. Sri Lanka in 1983 and 101 Herschelle Gibbs South Africa vs. Australia in 1999
Best bowling	7-51	Winston Davis West Indies vs. Australia in 1983

Five wickets in an innings	5	Winston Davis 7-51 West Indies vs. Australia 1983; 6-14 Gary Gilmour Australia vs. England in 1975; 5-34 Dennis Lillee Australia vs. Pakistan in 1975; 5-39 Ashantha de Mel Sri Lanka vs. Pakistan in 1983 and 5-44 Abdul Qadir Pakistan vs. Sri Lanka in 1983
Highest partnership	144	Imran Khan & Shahid Mahboob Pakistan vs. Sri Lanka in 1983 for the sixth wicket

2019 schedule	
21 June	England vs. Sri Lanka
29 June	Pakistan vs. Afghanistan
4 July	Afghanistan vs. West Indies
6 July	Sri Lanka vs. India

LORD'S

The Home of Cricket was the first ground to celebrate 100 Tests and additionally has overseen 61 ODIs since 1972. Middlesex's famous headquarters has also hosted four World Cup finals, the most of any ground, and will add a fifth in 2019 in addition to four other matches. It will be the dream of all participants to appear in the 14 July final. After recent redevelopment, Lord's can now accommodate 30,000 spectators.

World Cup matches hosted	10	
Highest total	334-4	England vs. India in 1975
Lowest completed total	132	Pakistan vs. Australia in 1999
Highest match aggregate	565-18	West Indies (291-8) vs. Australia (274) in 1975
Lowest match aggregate	265-12	Pakistan (132) vs. Australia (133-2) in 1999
Highest score	138*	Viv Richards West Indies vs. England in 1979
Centuries	5	Viv Richards 138* West Indies vs. England 1979; Dennis Amiss 137 England vs. India in 1975; 132* Neil Johnson Zimbabwe vs. Australia in 1999; 104 Mark Waugh Australia vs. Zimbabwe in 1999 and 102 Clive Lloyd West Indies vs. Australia in 1975
Best bowling	5-38	Joel Garner West Indies vs. England in 1979

Five wickets in an innings	2	Joel Garner 5-38 West Indies vs. England 1979 and Gary Gilmour 5-48 Australia vs. West Indies in 1975
Highest partnership	176	Dennis Amiss & Keith Fletcher England vs. India in 1975 for the second wicket

2019 schedule	
23 June	Pakistan vs. South Africa
25 June	England vs. Australia
29 June	New Zealand vs. Australia (d/n)
5 July	Pakistan vs. Bangladesh
14 July	Final

OLD TRAFFORD

A venue which has hosted all formats of international cricket, Lancashire's Old Trafford also holds the distinction of being the first ground used for ODIs in England. In addition to being the third-most used Test venue in England, the ground has also held forty-six ODIs since its debut in 1972. The ground can hold 26,000.

World Cup matches hosted	11	
Highest total	262-8	India vs. West Indies in 1983
Lowest completed total	45	Canada vs. England in 1979
Highest match aggregate	490-18	India (262-8) vs. West Indies (228) in 1983
Lowest match aggregate	91-12	Canada (45) vs. England (46-2) in 1979
Highest score	114*	Glenn Turner New Zealand vs. India in 1975
Centuries	2	Glenn Turner 114* New Zealand vs. India 1975 and Saeed Anwar 113* Pakistan vs. New Zealand in 1999
Best bowling	5-14	Glenn McGrath Australia vs. West Indies in 1999
Five wickets in an innings	2	Glenn McGrath 5-14 Australia vs. West Indies 1999 and Venkatesh Prasad 5-27 India vs. Pakistan in 1999
Highest partnership	194	Saeed Anwar & Wajahatullah Wasti Pakistan vs. New Zealand in 1999 for the first wicket

2019 schedule	
16 June	India vs. Pakistan
18 June	England vs. Afghanistan
22 June	West Indies vs. New Zealand (d/n)
27 June	West Indies vs. India
6 July	Australia vs. South Africa (d/n)
9 July	First semi-final 1st vs. 4th

SOUTHAMPTON

Hampshire's impressive ground first saw international action in 2003. It has been a regular venue for Test, T20 Internationals – England's first-ever game was held there in 2005 – and ODIs. Five World Cup games are scheduled to add to the twenty-two ODIs already held there. Three World Cup matches have been held in Southampton, but all were at the Northlands Road ground and the figures below relate to that ground, not the current one. The ground can accommodate 25,000.

World Cup matches hosted	3	
Highest total	275-8	Sri Lanka vs Kenya in 1999
Lowest completed total	156	New Zealand vs. West Indies in 1999
Highest match aggregate	512-17	Australia (272-7) vs Zimbabwe (240) in 1983
Lowest match aggregate	314-13	New Zealand (156) vs. West Indies (158-3) in 1999.
Highest score	84	Dave Houghton Zimbabwe vs Australia in 1983
Centuries	0	
Best bowling	4-46	Merv Dillon West Indies vs New Zealand in 1999
Five wickets in an innings	0	
Highest partnership	161	Maurice Odumbe & Alpesh Vadher Kenya vs Sri Lanka in 1999 for the sixth wicket

2019 schedule	
5 June	South Africa vs. India
10 June	South Africa vs. West Indies
14 June	England vs. West Indies
22 June	India vs. Afghanistan
24 June	Bangladesh vs. Afghanistan

TAUNTON

Somerset's main ground is a rarity amongst England's venues being the only one in the 2019 tournament which has hosted World Cup matches only. The ground has held many Women's ODIs over recent years. The picturesque ground will be doubling its existing tally of World Cup matches in the 2019 tournament and can hold up to 12,500 on international match days.

World Cup matches hosted	3	
Highest total	373-6	India vs. Sri Lanka in 1999
Lowest completed total	216	Sri Lanka vs. India in 1999
Highest match aggregate	619-19	England (333-9) vs. Sri Lanka (286) in 1983
Lowest match aggregate	460-12	Kenya (229-7) vs. Zimbabwe (231-5) in 1999
Highest score	183	Sourav Ganguly India vs. Sri Lanka in 1999
Centuries	3	Sourav Ganguly 183 India vs. Sri Lanka 1999; Rahul Dravid 145 India vs. Sri Lanka in 1999 and 130 David Gower England vs. Sri Lanka 1983
Best bowling	5-31	Robin Singh India vs. Sri Lanka in 1999
Five wickets in an innings	2	Robin Singh 5-31 India vs. Sri Lanka 1999 and Vic Marks 5-39 England vs. Sri Lanka 1983
Highest partnership	318	Sourav Ganguly & Rahul Dravid India vs. Sri Lanka in 1999 for the second wicket

2019 schedule	
8 June	Afghanistan vs. New Zealand (d/n)
12 June	Australia vs. Pakistan
17 June	West Indies vs. Bangladesh

THE OVAL

Along with Lord's, The Oval is only the second English ground to host over 100 Tests. Additionally, it has held the most ODIs of an English ground, sixty-seven, and five games will be held at the famous South London venue during the World Cup. Its first ODI was held in 1973 and the ground capacity is 25,500.

World Cup matches hosted	10	
Highest total	328-5	Australia vs. Sri Lanka in 1975
Lowest completed total	103	England vs. South Africa in 1999
Highest match aggregate	604-9	Australia (328-5) vs. Sri Lanka (276-4) in 1975
Lowest match aggregate	317-15	New Zealand (158) vs. West Indies (159-5) in 1975
Highest score	119	Viv Richards West Indies vs. India in 1983
Centuries	5	Viv Richards 119 West Indies vs. India 1983; 103 Saeed Anwar Pakistan vs. Zimbabwe in 1999; 102 Allan Lamb England vs. New Zealand in 1983; 101 Alan Turner Australia vs. Sri Lanka in 1975 and 100* Ajay Jadeja India vs. Australia in 1999
Best bowling	4-17	Allan Donald South Africa vs. England in 1999
Five wickets in an innings	0	
Highest partnership	182	Alan Turner & Rick McCosker Australia vs. Sri Lanka in 1975 for the first wicket

2019 schedule	
30 May	England vs. South Africa
2 June	South Africa vs. Bangladesh
5 June	Bangladesh vs. New Zealand (d/n)
9 June	India vs. Australia
15 June	Sri Lanka vs. Australia

TRENT BRIDGE

Nottinghamshire's headquarters first hosted an ODI in 1974 as well as all formats of international cricket. The ground has hosted 44 ODIs to date and its ground capacity is 17,500.

World Cup matches hosted	11	
Highest total	330-6	Pakistan vs. Sri Lanka in 1975
Lowest completed total	138	Sri Lanka vs. Pakistan in 1975
Highest match aggregate	511-13	Pakistan (261-3) vs. New Zealand (250) in 1983
Lowest match aggregate	335-11	Zimbabwe (167-8) vs. England (168-3) in 1999
Highest score	131	Keith Fletcher England vs. New Zealand in 1975
Centuries	3	Keith Fletcher 131 England vs. New Zealand 1975; 110 Trevor Chappell Australia vs. India in 1983 and 103* Zaheer Abbas Pakistan vs New Zealand in 1983
Best bowling	6-39	Ken MacLeay Australia vs. India in 1983
Five wickets in an innings	2	Ken MacLeay 6-39 Australia vs. India 1983 and Kapil Dev 5-43 India vs. Australia 1983
Highest partnership	159	Sadiq Mohammad & Majid Khan Pakistan vs. Sri Lanka in 1975 for the first wicket

2019 schedule	
31 May	West Indies vs. Pakistan
3 June	England vs. Pakistan
6 June	Australia vs. West Indies
13 June	India vs. New Zealand
20 June	Australia vs. Bangladesh

PLAYERS TO WATCH

Squads for the 2019 World Cup have not yet been released so I am rather keeping my fingers crossed that the names below who I fancy may do well will not a) fall lame, b) lose form but hope, most importantly, that they will be selected.

There is a feeling based on recent form that ENGLAND have a real chance of lifting the trophy for the first time with AUSTRALIA, INDIA and SOUTH AFRICA all very much in the frame.

ENGLAND's recent dominant and aggressive batting means that vast totals are very possible and, should JASON ROY get going, a rollicking start could be anticipated. JOS BUTTLER is proving to be a reliable wicket-keeper but spectators will be salivating at his potential in the middle order with the bat after many fine performances in the last year. BEN STOKES with bat and ball should be expected to also feature prominently as could MOEEN ALI with his aggressive batting and spin-bowling.

Despite having not yet reached a final, SOUTH AFRICA have many impressive players who will give their team a fine chance. QUINTON DE KOCK is another in the burgeoning list of destructive wicket-keeper batsmen whilst CHRIS MORRIS offers much with bat and ball and both have the ability to be crowd-pleasers. In KAGISO RABADA, South Africa have a bowler of rare potential and speed whilst AIDEN MARKRAM has the potential to succeed in all formats of the game.

INDIA can be expected to be potentially strong contenders and have in captain VIRAT KOHLI one of the finest batsmen in world cricket in all formats. M.S. DHONI is still one of the best ODI finishers and his experience will be vital. India has, in HARDIK PANDYA, a formidable all-rounder whilst in KULDEEP YADAV, they have that rare breed, a slow left-arm Chinaman bowler who has tasted significant success already.

AUSTRALIA's recent ODI record has been poor but this has happened before previous World Cups and they will expect to send a team which will give a chance of retaining their 2015 trophy. GLENN MAXWELL is an exciting batsman and with a potentially very fast bowling attack which could include PAT CUMMINS, MITCHELL STARC (the 2015 player of the tournament) and BILLY STANLAKE, Australia cannot be underestimated.

NEW ZEALAND have a very fine World Cup record despite, like England, never winning the main prize. Captain KANE WILLIAMSON is one of the finest batsmen in all formats and ROSS TAYLOR also has a very fine record and both will hope to continue their successes. The experienced TIM SOUTHEE should prove a handful with the ball as well as providing late-order runs whilst TRENT BOULT, not dissimilar in style to Geoff Allott who did so well in the 1999 World Cup in England, can add to his reputation.

PAKISTAN also have the ability to do well. Their captain and wicket-keeper, SARFRAZ AHMED, is a fine performer as is fast bowler, MOHAMMAD AMIR. He could be well supported by JUNAID KHAN and opener IMAM-UL-HAQ has been in the runs recently.

SRI LANKA have not enjoyed great success just recently but the experience of ANGELO MATHEWS, despite recently being dropped, will surely help if he is selected. LASITH MALINGA's fine World Cup record will be a boost for Sri Lanka whilst NIROSHAN DICKWELLA has performed creditably as opener recently.

WEST INDIES enjoyed a tremendous record in the first three World Cups which were all held in England. Although their record since has not been as enviable, they still have a competitive team and captain JASON HOLDER has proved to be a fine bowler who makes good runs lower down. Many spectators will remember SHAI HOPE's fine batting in England in 2017 and he could provide the backbone to the batting. KEMAR ROACH has fine pace and could hurry batsmen up whilst CARLOS BRATHWAITE should entertain with bat and ball. CHRIS GAYLE will hope for one last hurrah before his ODI retirement after the World Cup.

BANGLADESH's World Cup record may still be modest but they are proving to be a decent ODI side which has performed well recently. Opening batsmen IMRUL KAYES and LITON DAS have made good runs of late and MAHMUDULLAH Bangladesh's sole World Cup centurion, promises much with bat and ball. MASHRAFE MORTAZA will provide experience with the ball whilst wicket-keeper MUSHFIQUR RAHIM has an impressive batting record.

AFGHANISTAN will play in their second World Cup and their form in the recent Asia Cup has seen them impress with wins over Sri Lanka, Bangladesh and a tie with India. Leg-spinner RASHID KHAN is a familiar name on the circuit and he and MOHAMMAD NABI should provide more experience. Wicket-keeper and opening batsman MOHAMMAD SHAHZAD has the ability to entertain spectators.

WORLD CUP FINAL STATISTICS

Finals	11
Highest total	359 for 2 in 50 overs Australia vs. India at Johannesburg in 2003
Highest successful run chase	277 for 4 in 48.2 overs India vs. Sri Lanka at Mumbai in 2011
Lowest completed total	132 in 39 overs Pakistan vs. Australia at Lord's in 1999
Highest match aggregate	593 for 12 wickets Australia (359-2) vs. India (234) at Johannesburg in 2003
Lowest match aggregate	265 for 12 wickets Pakistan (132) vs. Australia (133-2) at Lord's in 1999
Biggest victory margins	125 runs Australia vs. India at Johannesburg in 2003
	8 wickets Australia vs. Pakistan at Lord's in 1999
Lowest victory margins	7 runs Australia vs. England at Calcutta in 1987
	6 wickets India vs. Sri Lanka at Mumbai in 2011
Highest score	149 Adam Gilchrist Australia vs. Sri Lanka at Bridgetown in 2007
Centuries	Adam Gilchrist 149 Australia vs. Sri Lanka at Bridgetown in 2007; 140* Ricky Ponting Australia vs. India at Johannesburg in 2003; 138* Viv Richards West Indies vs. England at Lord's in 1979; 107* Aravinda de Silva Sri Lanka vs. Australia at Lahore in 1996; 103* Mahela Jayawardene Sri Lanka vs. India at Mumbai in 2011 and 102 Clive Lloyd West Indies vs. Australia at Lord's in 1975

Best bowling	11-0-38-5 Joel Garner West Indies vs. England at Lord's in 1979
Five wickets in an innings	Joel Garner 5-38 West Indies vs. England at Lord's in 1979 and Gary Gilmour 5-48 Australia vs. West Indies at Lord's in 1975
Finals won by side batting first	7
Finals won by side batting second	4
Most appearances	4 Ricky Ponting & Glenn McGrath (both Australia)

PREVIOUS FINALS

1975	WEST INDIES (291-8) beat AUSTRALIA (274) by 17 runs at Lord's
1979	WEST INDIES (286-9) beat ENGLAND (194) by 92 runs at Lord's
1983	INDIA (183) beat WEST INDIES (140) by 43 runs at Lord's
1987	AUSTRALIA (253-5) beat ENGLAND (246-8) by 7 runs at Calcutta
1992	PAKISTAN (249-6) beat ENGLAND (227) by 22 runs at Melbourne
1996	SRI LANKA (245-3) beat AUSTRALIA (241-7) by 7 wickets at Lahore
1999	AUSTRALIA (133-2) beat PAKISTAN (132) by 8 wickets at Lord's
2003	AUSTRALIA (359-2) beat INDIA (234) by 125 runs at Johannesburg
2007	AUSTRALIA (281-4) beat SRI LANKA (215-8) by 53 runs at Bridgetown
2011	INDIA (277-4) beat SRI LANKA (274-6) by 6 wickets at Mumbai
2015	AUSTRALIA (186-3) beat NEW ZEALAND (183) by 7 wickets at Melbourne

LORD'S FINALS WORLD CUP RECORDS

Finals	4
Highest total	291-8 West Indies vs. Australia in 1975
Lowest completed total	132 Pakistan vs. Australia in 1999
Highest match aggregate	565-18 West Indies (291-8) vs. Australia (274) in 1975
Lowest match aggregate	265-12 Pakistan (132) vs. Australia (133-2) in 1999

Biggest victory margins	92 runs West Indies (286-9) vs. England (194) in 1979
	8 wickets Australia (133-2) vs. Pakistan (132) in 1999
Lowest victory margin	17 runs West Indies (291-8) vs. Australia (274) in 1975
Highest score	138* Viv Richards West Indies vs. England in 1979
Centuries	Viv Richards 138* West Indies vs. England 1979 and Clive Lloyd 102 West Indies vs. Australia 1975
Best bowling	5-38 Joel Garner West Indies vs. England in 1979
Five wickets in an innings	Joel Garner 5-38 West Indies vs. England at Lord's in 1979 and Gary Gilmour 5-48 Australia vs. West Indies at Lord's in 1975
Highest partnership	149 Rohan Kanhai & Clive Lloyd West Indies vs. Australia in 1975 for the fourth wicket
Finals won by side batting first	3 West Indies vs. Australia in 1975; West Indies vs. England in 1979 and India vs. West Indies in 1983
Finals won by side batting second	1 Australia vs. Pakistan in 1999

LORD'S FINALS MISCELLANY

* The three highest scores in Lord's finals have all been by West Indies: 138* by Viv Richards in 1979; 102 by Clive Lloyd in 1975 and 86 by Collis King in 1979.
* The two five-wicket hauls in World Cup matches at Lord's have both been in finals.
* The toss has been won in each final by the side which lost.
* Viv Richards holds the record for most runs in finals at one venue (176) which is Lord's.

WORLD CUP STATISTICS
1975–2015

GENERAL TEAM RECORDS

HIGHEST TOTALS	
417 for 6 in 50 overs	Australia vs. Afghanistan at Perth in 2015
413 for 5 in 50 overs	India vs. Bermuda at Port of Spain in 2007
411 for 4 in 50 overs	South Africa vs. Ireland at Canberra in 2015
408 for 5 in 50 overs	South Africa vs. West Indies at Sydney in 2015
398 for 5 in 50 overs	Sri Lanka vs. Kenya at Kandy in 1996

HIGHEST SUCCESSFUL CHASES	
329 for 7 in 49.1 overs	Ireland vs. England at Bangalore in 2011
322 for 4 in 48.1 overs	Bangladesh vs. Scotland at Nelson in 2015
313 for 7 in 49.2 overs	Sri Lanka vs. Zimbabwe at New Plymouth in 1992
312 for 1 in 47.2 overs	Sri Lanka vs. England at Wellington in 2015
307 for 4 in 47.4 overs	Ireland vs. Netherlands at Kolkata in 2011
307 for 6 in 45.5 overs	Ireland vs West Indies at Nelson in 2015

HIGHEST TOTALS WITHOUT A CENTURY	
341 for 6 in 50 overs	South Africa vs. United Arab Emirates at Wellington in 2015
339 for 6 in 50 overs	Pakistan vs. United Arab Emirates at Napier in 2015
338 for 5 in 60 overs	Pakistan vs. Sri Lanka at Swansea in 1983
331 for 6 in 50 overs	New Zealand vs. Sri Lanka at Christchurch in 2015
331 for 7 in 50 overs	New Zealand vs. Kenya at Gros Islet in 2007
There have been 21 occasions of 300 plus being scored without an individual century	

LOWEST TOTALS IN FAILED CHASES WITH RESULTS WHERE TARGET WAS 175 OR FEWER	
125	England vs. Zimbabwe (134) at Albury in 1992
105 for 7	Zimbabwe vs. New Zealand (162-3) at Napier in 1992
104 for 1	Zimbabwe (target 159) vs. India (203-7) at Hamilton in 1992
151	Pakistan vs. England (165-9) at Leeds in 1975
93	West Indies vs. Kenya (166) at Pune in 1996
165	South Africa vs. England (171) at Chennai in 2011

CLOSEST RESULTS	
Tied match	Australia (213) vs. South Africa (213) at Birmingham in 1999
Tied match	Sri Lanka (268-9) vs. South Africa (229-6) at Durban in 2003
Tied match	Ireland (221-9) vs. Zimbabwe (221) at Kingston in 2007
Tied match	India (338) vs. England (338-8) at Bangalore in 2011
There have been six occasions of one-wicket victories	
1 run	Australia (270-6) vs. India (269) at Madras in 1987
1 run	Australia (237-9) vs. India (234) at Brisbane in 1992

HIGHEST MATCH AGGREGATES	
688 for 18 wickets	Australia (376-9) vs. Sri Lanka (312-9) at Sydney in 2015
676 for 18 wickets	India (338) vs. England (338-8) at Bangalore in 2011
671 for 16 wickets	Australia (377-6) vs. South Africa (294) at Basseterre 2007
661 for 12 wickets	West Indies (372-2) vs. Zimbabwe (289) at Canberra in 2015
657 for 18 wickets	Ireland (331-8) vs. Zimbabwe (326) at Hobart in 2015

LOWEST MATCH AGGREGATES WITH RESULT	
73 for 11 wickets	Canada (36) vs. Sri Lanka (37-1) at Paarl in 2003
91 for 12 wickets	Canada (45) vs. England (46-2) at Manchester in 1979
117 for 11 wickets	Bangladesh (58) vs. West Indies (59-1) at Dhaka in 2011
138 for 12 wickets	Scotland (68) vs. West Indies (70-2) at Leicester in 1999
141 for 10 wickets	Kenya (69) vs. New Zealand (72-0) at Chennai in 2011

MOST CONSECUTIVE MATCHES WITHOUT VICTORY	
18	Zimbabwe between 11 June 1983 and 14 March 1992
14	Scotland from 16 May 1999 to date
14	Scotland from 16 May 1999 to 14 March 2015

MOST CONSECUTIVE MATCHES WITHOUT DEFEAT	
34	Australia between 27 May 1999 and 16 March 2011
11	India between 20 March 2011 and 19 March 2015

MOST SCORES OF FIFTY IN AN INNINGS
There have been 12 occasions of four scores of 50 in the same innings

MOST BOUNDARIES SCORED BY TEAMS IN AN INNINGS	
57 (43 x 4, 14 x 6)	Sri Lanka (398-5) vs. Kenya at Kandy in 1996
54 (39 x 4, 15 x 6)	New Zealand (393-6) vs. West Indies at Wellington in 2015
51 (40 x 4, 11 x 6)	Australia (377-6) vs. South Africa at Basseterre in 2007
50 (36 x 4, 14 x 6)	Australia (417-6) vs. Afghanistan at Perth in 2015
49 (37 x 4, 12 x 6)	South Africa (411-4) vs. Ireland at Canberra in 2015

MOST DUCKS IN AN INNINGS	
5	England vs. West Indies at Lord's in 1979
5	Canada vs. Sri Lanka at Paarl in 2003
5	Sri Lanka vs. India at Johannesburg in 2003
5	Bermuda vs. India at Port of Spain in 2007
5	Ireland vs. Sri Lanka at St. George's in 2007
5	Scotland vs. New Zealand at Dunedin in 2015
5	Scotland vs. Australia at Hobart in 2015

MOST EXTRAS IN AN INNINGS	
59	Pakistan (261-6) vs. Scotland at Chester-le-Street in 1999
51	Zimbabwe (252-9) vs. India at Leicester in 1999
47	New Zealand (241-7) vs. Pakistan at Manchester in 1999
46	Pakistan (317-7) vs. Kenya at Hambantota in 2011
44	Kenya (235-7) vs. India at Bristol in 1999
44	Bangladesh (185-9) vs. Scotland at Edinburgh in 1999

OCCASIONS OF CHAMPIONS LOSING EARLIER IN THE SAME TOURNAMENT TO THEIR FINAL OPPONENTS	
1983	India lost to West Indies at The Oval #
1999	Australia lost to Pakistan at Leeds
2015	Australia lost to New Zealand at Auckland
# Additionally in 1983, India also beat West Indies at Manchester before the final	

BATTING RECORDS

MOST CAREER RUNS	
2278 (average 56.95 with six centuries)	Sachin Tendulkar (India)
1743 (average 45.87 with five centuries)	Ricky Ponting (Australia)
1532 (average 56.74 with five centuries)	Kumar Sangakkara (Sri Lanka)
1225 (average 42.24 with two centuries)	Brian Lara (West Indies)
1207 (average 63.53 with four centuries)	Abraham de Villiers (South Africa)
Seventeen batsmen have scored over 1000 World Cup runs	

MOST TOURNAMENT RUNS	
673 (average 61.18)	Sachin Tendulkar (India) in 2003
659 (average 73.22)	Matthew Hayden (Australia) in 2007
548 (average 60.89)	Mahela Jayawardene (Sri Lanka) in 2007
547 (average 68.38)	Martin Guptill (New Zealand) in 2015
541 (average 108.20)	Kumar Sangakkara (Sri Lanka) in 2015
There have been eight occasions of players scoring 500 runs in a tournament. Sachin Tendulkar has done so twice.	

HIGHEST SCORES	
237*	Martin Guptill New Zealand vs. West Indies at Wellington in 2015
215	Chris Gayle West Indies vs. Zimbabwe at Canberra in 2015
188*	Gary Kirsten South Africa vs. United Arab Emirates at Rawalpindi in 1996
183	Sourav Ganguly India vs. Sri Lanka at Taunton in 1999
181	Viv Richards West Indies vs. Sri Lanka at Karachi in 1987

HIGHEST SCORES IN A LOSING TEAM	
156	Kyle Coetzer Scotland vs. Bangladesh at Nelson in 2015
143	Herschelle Gibbs South Africa vs. New Zealand at Johannesburg in 2003
142	Dave Houghton Zimbabwe vs. New Zealand at Hyderabad in 1987
141	Scott Styris New Zealand vs. Sri Lanka at Bloemfontein in 2003
138	Brendan Taylor Zimbabwe vs. India at Auckland in 2015
In total, there have been 31 centuries scored in a losing cause	

MOST CENTURIES IN A TOURNAMENT	
4	Kumar Sangakkara (Sri Lanka) in 2015
3	Mark Waugh (Australia) in 1996
3	Sourav Ganguly (India) in 2003
3	Matthew Hayden (Australia) in 2007

CARRYING BAT THROUGH COMPLETED INNINGS

49*	Ridley Jacobs West Indies vs. Australia at Manchester in 1999

This excludes those who have batted through the allotted overs but where their side was not dismissed

MOST DUCKS IN A CAREER

5	Nathan Astle (New Zealand)
5	Ijaz Ahmed (Pakistan)

MOST CONSECUTIVE DUCKS

3	Shem Ngoche (Kenya)
3	Nicholas de Groot (Canada)

MOST CONSECUTIVE INNINGS WITHOUT A DUCK

37	Sanath Jayasuriya (Sri Lanka)
36	Ricky Ponting (Australia)
31	Brian Lara (West Indies)
30	Steve Waugh (Australia)

HIGHEST SCORE AT EACH BATTING POSITION

1	237*	Martin Guptill New Zealand vs. West Indies at Wellington in 2015
2	215	Chris Gayle West Indies vs. Zimbabwe at Canberra in 2015
3	145	Rahul Dravid India vs. Sri Lanka at Taunton in 1999
4	181	Viv Richards West Indies vs. Sri Lanka at Karachi in 1987
5	162*	Abraham de Villiers South Africa vs. West Indies at Sydney in 2015
6	175*	Kapil Dev India vs. Zimbabwe at Tunbridge Wells in 1983
7	89	Darren Sammy West Indies vs. Ireland at Nelson in 2015
8	72*	Heath Streak Zimbabwe vs. New Zealand at Bloemfontein in 2003
9	64	Andy Bichel Australia vs. New Zealand at Port Elizabeth in 2003
10	48*	Daren Powell West Indies vs. South Africa at St. George's in 2007
11	43	Shoaib Akhtar Pakistan vs. England at Cape Town in 2003

MOST INDIVIDUAL BOUNDARIES (4&6) IN AN INNINGS

35 (11 x 6, 24 x 4)	Martin Guptill (237*) New Zealand vs. West Indies at Wellington in 2015
26 (16 x 6, 10 x 4)	Chris Gayle (215) West Indies vs. Zimbabwe at Canberra in 2015

MOST INDIVIDUAL BOUNDARIES (4&6) IN AN INNINGS	
25 (8 x 6, 17 x 4)	Abraham de Villiers South Africa vs. West Indies at Sydney in 2015
24 (5 x 6, 19 x 4)	David Warner Australia vs. Afghanistan at Perth in 2015
24 (7 x 6, 17 x 4)	Sourav Ganguly India vs. Sri Lanka at Taunton in 1999

BOWLING RECORDS

MOST CAREER WICKETS	
71 (average 18.20)	Glenn McGrath (Australia)
68 (average 19.63)	Muttiah Muralitharan (Sri Lanka)
55 (average 23.84)	Wasim Akram (Pakistan)
49 (average 21.22)	Chaminda Vaas (Sri Lanka)
44 (average 20.23)	Zaheer Khan (India)
44 (average 27.82)	Javagal Srinath (India)

MOST TOURNAMENT WICKETS	
26 (average 13.73)	Glenn McGrath (Australia) in 2007
23 (average 14.39)	Chaminda Vaas (Sri Lanka) in 2003
23 (average 15.26)	Muttiah Muralitharan (Sri Lanka) in 2007
23 (average 20.30)	Shaun Tait (Australia) in 2007

BEST BOWLING PERFORMANCES	
7-4-15-7	Glenn McGrath Australia vs. Namibia at Potchefstroom in 2003
10-0-20-7	Andy Bichel Australia vs. England at Port Elizabeth in 2003
9-0-33-7	Tim Southee New Zealand vs. England at Wellington 2015
10.3-0-51-7	Winston Davis West Indies vs. Australia at Leeds in 1983
12-6-14-6	Gary Gilmour Australia vs. England at Leeds in 1975

FIVE WICKETS IN AN INNINGS
There have been 54 occasions of a bowler taking five or more wickets in an innings

BEST BOWLING IN A LOSING TEAM	
10-2-23-6	Shane Bond New Zealand vs. Australia at Port Elizabeth in 2003
9-0-28-6	Mitchell Starc Australia vs. New Zealand at Auckland in 2015
10-1-35-5	Saqlain Mushtaq Pakistan vs. Bangladesh at Northampton in 1999
12-1-39-5	Ashantha de Mel Sri Lanka vs. Pakistan at Leeds in 1983

BEST BOWLING IN A LOSING TEAM	
12-2-43-5	Kapil Dev India vs. Australia at Nottingham in 1983
10-2-43-5	Rudi van Vuuren Namibia vs. England at Port Elizabeth in 2003

HAT-TRICKS	
10-2-51-3	Chetan Sharma India vs. New Zealand at Nagpur in 1987
6.3-1-16-3	Saqlain Mushtaq Pakistan vs. Zimbabwe at The Oval in 1999
9.1-2-25-6	Chaminda Vaas Sri Lanka vs. Bangladesh at Pietermaritzburg in 2003
8-3-14-3	Brett Lee Australia vs. Kenya at Durban in 2003
9.2-0-54-4	Lasith Malinga Sri Lanka vs. South Africa at Providence in 2007 #
8.3-0-27-6	Kemar Roach West Indies vs. Netherlands at Delhi in 2011
7.4-0-38-6	Lasith Malinga Sri Lanka vs. Kenya at Colombo in 2011
10-0-71-5	Steven Finn England vs. Australia at Melbourne in 2015
9-1-29-3	Jean-Paul Duminy South Africa vs. Sri Lanka at Sydney in 2015
# Malinga's figures against South Africa include four wickets in four balls	

INDIVIDUAL RECORDS

MOST APPEARANCES	
46	Ricky Ponting (Australia)
45	Sachin Tendulkar (India)
40	Mahela Jayawardene (Sri Lanka)
40	Muttiah Muralitharan (Sri Lanka)
39	Glenn McGrath (Australia)

CAPTAINCY RECORDS

MOST MATCHES AS CAPTAIN	
29	Ricky Ponting (Australia)
27	Stephen Fleming (New Zealand)
23	Mohammad Azharuddin (India)
22	Imran Khan (Pakistan)
17	Graeme Smith (South Africa)
17	Mahendra Singh Dhoni (India)
17	Clive Lloyd (West Indies)

MOST WINS	
26	Ricky Ponting (Australia)
16	Stephen Fleming (New Zealand)
15	Clive Lloyd (West Indies)
14	Imran Khan (Pakistan)
14	Mahendra Singh Dhoni (India)

MOST CAREER RUNS	
1160 (average 52.73)	Ricky Ponting (Australia)
882 (average 36.75)	Stephen Fleming (New Zealand)
636 (average 35.33)	Mohammad Azharuddin (India)
626 (average 39.13)	Graeme Smith (South Africa)
615 (average 38.44)	Imran Khan (Pakistan)

MOST TOURNAMENT RUNS	
548 (average 60.89)	Mahela Jayawardene (Sri Lanka) in 2007
539 (average 67.38)	Ricky Ponting (Australia) in 2007
482 (average 96.40)	Abraham de Villiers (South Africa) in 2015
465 (average 93.00)	Kumar Sangakkara (Sri Lanka) in 2011
465 (average 58.13)	Sourav Ganguly (India) in 2003

HIGHEST SCORES	
181	Viv Richards West Indies vs. Sri Lanka at Karachi in 1987
175*	Kapil Dev India vs. Zimbabwe at Tunbridge Wells in 1983
171*	Glenn Turner New Zealand vs. East Africa at Birmingham in 1975
162*	Abraham de Villiers South Africa vs. West Indies at Sydney in 2015
158	Andrew Strauss England vs. India at Bangalore in 2011

MOST CAREER WICKETS	
24 (average 19.71)	Imran Khan (Pakistan)
21 (average 12.86)	Shahid Afridi (Pakistan)
18 (average 26.50)	Wasim Akram (Pakistan)
17 (average 29.65)	Kapil Dev (India)
13 (average 23.00)	Steve Tikolo (Kenya)

BEST BOWLING IN AN INNINGS		
8-3-16-5	Shahid Afridi	Pakistan vs. Kenya at Hambantota in 2011
10-0-23-5	Shahid Afridi	Pakistan vs. Canada at Colombo in 2011
12-2-43-5	Kapil Dev	India vs. Australia at Nottingham in 1983

MOST TOURNAMENT WICKETS	
21 (average 12.86)	Shahid Afridi (Pakistan) in 2011
17 (average 13.06)	Imran Khan (Pakistan) in 1987
15 (average 22.80)	Wasim Akram (Pakistan) in 1999
12 (average 20.42)	Kapil Dev (India) in 1983
11 (average 18.73)	Bob Willis (England) in 1983

FIELDING RECORDS

MOST CATCHES IN A MATCH		
4	Mohammad Kaif	India vs. Sri Lanka at Johannesburg in 2003
4	Soumya Sarkar	Bangladesh vs. Scotland at Nelson in 2015
4	Umar Akmal	Pakistan vs. Ireland at Adelaide in 2015

MOST TOURNAMENT CATCHES	
11	Ricky Ponting (Australia) in 2003
9	Rilee Rossouw (South Africa) in 2015
Nine other players have taken eight catches in a tournament	

MOST CAREER CATCHES	
28 (in 46 matches)	Ricky Ponting (Australia)
18 (in 38 matches)	Sanath Jayasuriya (Sri Lanka)
16 (in 28 matches)	Chris Cairns (New Zealand)
16 (in 34 matches)	Brian Lara (West Indies)
16 (in 35 matches)	Inzamam-ul-Haq (Pakistan)
16 (in 40 matches)	Mahela Jayawardene (Sri Lanka)
All catching records apply to fielders only and not wicket-keepers	

WICKET-KEEPING RECORDS

MOST MATCH DISMISSALS

6	Adam Gilchrist Australia vs. Namibia at Potchefstoom in 2003
6	Sarfraz Ahmed Pakistan vs. South Africa at Auckland in 2015
There have been eight occasions of five or more dismissals in an innings	

MOST TOURNAMENT DISMISSALS

21 (all catches)	Adam Gilchrist (Australia) in 2003
17 (15 catches & 2 stumpings)	Kumar Sangakkara (Sri Lanka) in 2003
17 (12 catches & 5 stumpings)	Adam Gilchrist (Australia) in 2007
16 (15 catches & 1 stumping)	Rahul Dravid (India) in 2003
16 (15 catches & 1 stumping)	Jeff Dujon (West Indies) in 1983
16 (12 catches & 4 stumpings)	Moin Khan (Pakistan) in 1999
16 (all catches)	Brad Haddin (Australia) in 2015

MOST CAREER DISMISSALS

54 (41 catches & 13 stumpings)	Kumar Sangakkara (Sri Lanka)
52 (45 catches & 7 stumpings)	Adam Gilchrist (Australia)
32 (30 catches & 2 stumpings)	Brendon McCullum (New Zealand)
32 (27 catches & 5 stumpings)	Mahendra Singh Dhoni (India)
31 (31 catches & 0 stumpings)	Mark Boucher (South Africa)

HIGHEST SCORES

149	Adam Gilchrist Australia vs. Sri Lanka at Bridgetown in 2007
145	Rahul Dravid India vs. Sri Lanka at Taunton in 1999
142	Dave Houghton Zimbabwe vs. New Zealand at Hyderabad in 1987
138	Brendan Taylor Zimbabwe vs. India at Auckland in 2015
134	Abraham de Villiers South Africa vs Netherlands at Mohali in 2011
There have been 15 centuries scored by wicket-keepers	

MOST TOURNAMENT RUNS	
541 (average 108.20)	Kumar Sangakkara (Sri Lanka) in 2015
465 (average 93.00)	Kumar Sangakkara (Sri Lanka) in 2011
453 (average 45.30)	Adam Gilchrist (Australia) in 2007
433 (average 72.17)	Brendan Taylor (Zimbabwe) in 2015
408 (average 40.80)	Adam Gilchrist (Australia) in 2003

MOST CAREER RUNS	
1532 (average 56.74)	Kumar Sangakkara (Sri Lanka)
1085 (average 36.17)	Adam Gilchrist (Australia)
520 (average 57.78)	Brendan Taylor (Zimbabwe)
520 (average 32.50)	Alec Stewart (England)
510 (average 31.88)	Mushfiqur Rahim (Bangladesh)
507 (average 42.25)	Mahendra Singh Dhoni (India)

PARTNERSHIPS

CENTURY PARTERSHIPS
There have been 264 century partnerships in the World Cup

HIGHEST PARTNERSHIP FOR EACH WICKET					
1	282	Upul Tharanga & Tillakaratne Dilshan	SL vs. Zim	Pallekele	2011
2	372	Chris Gayle & Marlon Samuels	WI vs. Zim.	Canberra	2015
3	237*	Rahul Dravid & Sachin Tendulkar	Ind. vs. Ken.	Bristol	1999
4	204	Michael Clarke & Brad Hodge	Aus. vs. Net.	Basseterre	2007
5	256*	David Miller & Jean-Paul Duminy	SA vs. Zim.	Hamilton	2015
6	162	Kevin O'Brien & Alex Cusack	Ire. vs. Eng.	Bangalore	2011
7	107	Amjad Javed & Nasir Aziz	UAE vs. WI	Napier	2015
	107	Shaiman Anwar & Amjad Javed	UAE vs. Ire.	Brisbane	2015
8	117	Dave Houghton & Iain Butchart	Zim. vs. NZ	Hyderabad	1987
9	126*	Kapil Dev & Syed Kirmani	Ind. vs. Zim.	Tunbridge Wells	1983
10	71	Andy Roberts & Joel Garner	WI vs. Ind.	Manchester	1983

LOWEST COMPLETED TOTALS TO INCLUDE A CENTURY PARTNERSHIP	
175	United Arab Emirates vs. West Indies at Napier in 2015
183	New Zealand vs. Australia at Melbourne in 2015
188	Zimbabwe vs. Sri Lanka at Pallekele in 2011
194	England vs. West Indies at Lord's in 1979

VENUE RECORDS

MOST MATCHES HOSTED	
12	Headingley, Leeds
11	Edgbaston, Birmingham
11	Trent Bridge, Nottingham
11	Old Trafford, Manchester
10	Lord's
10	The Oval
10	Melbourne

VENUES WITH MOST RUNS SCORED	
4972	Trent Bridge, Nottingham
4564	Melbourne
4515	Edgbaston
4468	The Oval

VENUES WITH MOST CENTURIES SCORED	
7	Melbourne
6	Karachi (National Stadium)

VENUES WITH MOST FIFTIES SCORED	
26	Trent Bridge, Nottingham
25	Melbourne
25	The Oval

VENUES WITH MOST DUCKS SCORED	
24	Edgbaston, Birmingham
22	Headingley, Leeds

MOST INDIVIDUAL CAREER RUNS AT ONE VENUE	
309	Gary Kirsten (South Africa) at Rawalpindi
275	Martin Crowe (New Zealand) at Eden Park, Auckland
271	Viv Richards (West Indies) at Lord's
270	Tillakaratne Dilshan (Sri Lanka) at R.Premadasa Stadium, Colombo

MOST INDIVIDUAL CAREER WICKETS AT ONE VENUE	
11	Andy Roberts (West Indies) at The Oval
10	Lasith Malinga (Sri Lanka) at R.Premadasa Stadium, Colombo
10	Shahid Afridi (Pakistan) at R.Premadasa Stadium, Colombo

VENUES WITH MOST MATCHES WITHOUT A CENTURY	
5	St. George's Park, Port Elizabeth
4	McLean Park, Napier

GENERAL PLAYER RECORDS

OLDEST PLAYERS	
47 years 257 days	Nolan Clarke (Netherlands)
44 years 306 days	John Traicos (Zimbabwe)
43 years 267 days	Khurram Khan (United Arab Emirates)
43 years 236 days	Lennie Louw (Namibia)
43 years 129 days	Flavian Aponso (Netherlands)

Dates are based on the last match on which the player was selected. In total, 18 players have appeared over the age of 40 of which the oldest Test cricketers are Sri Lanka's Somachandra de Silva (41 years 9 days); Pakistan's Misbah-ul-Haq (40 years 296 days) and Lance Gibbs of West Indies (40 years 251 days). Omar Henry (40 years 39 days) would later make his Test debut for South Africa.

ALL ROUND RECORDS

FIFTY RUNS AND FOUR OR MORE WICKETS IN A MATCH	
Duncan Fletcher 69* and 4-42	Zimbabwe vs. Australia at Nottingham in 1983
Ian Botham 53 and 4-31	England vs. Australia at Sydney in 1992
Neil Johnson 59 and 4-42	Zimbabwe vs. Kenya at Taunton in 1999
Maurice Odumbe 52* and 4-38	Kenya vs. Bangladesh at Johannesburg in 2003
Feiko Kloppenburg 121 and 4-42	Netherlands vs. Namibia at Bloemfontein in 2003
Yuvraj Singh 50* and 5-31	India vs. Ireland at Bangalore in 2011
Tillakaratne Dilshan 144 and 4-4	Sri Lanka vs. Zimbabwe at Pallekele in 2011
Wahab Riaz 54* and 4-45	Pakistan vs. Zimbabwe at Brisbane in 2015

BEST CAREER FIGURES	(Min 500 runs & 25 wickets)
Imran Khan (Pakistan)	666 runs (average 35.05) and 34 wickets (average 19.26)
Sanath Jayasuriya (Sri Lanka)	1165 runs (average 34.26) and 27 wickets (average 39.26)
Kapil Dev (India)	669 runs (average 37.17) and 28 wickets (average 31.86)
Steve Waugh (Australia)	978 runs (average 48.90) and 27 wickets (average 30.15)

ASSOCIATE RECORDS

HIGHEST SCORES BY ASSOCIATE COUNTRIES AGAINST TEST PLAYING NATIONS		
156	Kyle Coetzer	Scotland vs. Bangladesh at Nelson in 2015
142	Dave Houghton	Zimbabwe vs. New Zealand at Hyderabad in 1987
119	Ryan ten Doeschate	Netherlands vs. England at Nagpur in 2011
115*	Andy Flower	Zimbabwe vs. Sri Lanka at New Plymouth in 1992
115*	Jeremy Bray	Ireland vs. Zimbabwe at Kingston, Jamaica in 2007

There have been nine instances of players from non-Test playing countries scoring centuries against Test playing nations. Scores above are before a country, if applicable, gained Test status.

MOST CAREER RUNS	
768 (average 29.54)	Steve Tikolo (Kenya)
627 (average 29.86)	William Porterfield (Ireland)
620 (average 32.63)	Niall O'Brien (Ireland)
567 (average 29.84)	Dave Houghton (Zimbabwe)
500 (average 29.41)	Ravindu Shah (Kenya)

MOST CAREER WICKETS	
23 (average 35.52)	Thomas Odoyo (Kenya)
18 (average 31.50)	Maurice Odumbe (Kenya)
17 (average 30.24)	John Davison (Canada)
16 (average 31.13)	Trent Johnston (Ireland)
16 (average 42.06)	John Traicos (Zimbabwe)

MOST CAREER APPEARANCES	
28	Steve Tikolo (Kenya)
25	Thomas Odoyo (Kenya)
21	William Porterfield (Ireland)
21	Niall O'Brien (Ireland)

WINS BY ASSOCIATE TEAMS OVER TEST PLAYING NATIONS
Sri Lanka beat India at Manchester in 1979
Zimbabwe beat Australia at Nottingham in 1983
Zimbabwe beat England at Albury in 1992
Kenya beat West Indies at Pune in 1996
Bangladesh beat Pakistan at Northampton in 1999
Kenya beat Sri Lanka at Nairobi in 2003
Kenya beat Bangladesh at Johannesburg in 2003
Kenya beat Zimbabwe at Bloemfontein in 2003
Canada beat Bangladesh at Durban in 2003
Ireland beat Pakistan at Kingston in 2007
Ireland beat Bangladesh at Bridgetown in 2007
Ireland beat England at Bangalore in 2011
Ireland beat West Indies at Nelson in 2015
Ireland beat Zimbabwe at Hobart in 2015
Associate record statistics are based on teams which have never played Test or before they achieved Test status

WORLD CUP QUIZ

All questions relate to performances in the World Cup only.
1) Which is the only English ground to see two individual bowling performances of six (or more) wickets in an innings?
2) How many ties have there been?
3) Which captain first hit the winning runs in a final?
4) Which three bowlers from non-Test playing countries took five wickets in an innings during the 2003 tournament?
5) Who made the highest score from a non-Test playing country?
6) Where did Pakistan's Shoaib Akhtar bowl the first officially-recorded 100mph delivery?
7) Which country has reached most semi-finals without winning a competition?
8) Which is the only Test country, which has not played Test Cricket, to reach a semi-final?
9) Which player (who went on to become a TV celebrity and MP) made his ODI debut in the 1987 Reliance World Cup and, despite passing 50, could not stop a one-run defeat for his team?
10) Which captains have scored centuries in finals?
11) Which English ground saw a 318-run partnership between India's Sourav Ganguly and Rahul Dravid against Sri Lanka?
12) Which country has participated in three World Cup tournaments but failed to win a match?
13) What is the lowest total made by a Test-playing country against a non-Test playing team?
14) Who is the only England player to open the batting and bowling in the same match?
15) Who is the only player to appear in three finals without being on the victorious side?
16) Which bowler has taken most wickets from a non-Test playing country?

17) Which captains have won the Man of the Match award in finals?
18) Which legendary batsman proved to be an effective bowler, bowling in all five of England's games in the 1979 World Cup but bowled only once in other ODIs?
19) Which feat did Aravinda de Silva perform in the 1996 final which no other player has achieved in a final?
20) Which feat did Australian batsmen Matthew Hayden, Andrew Symonds and Darren Lehmann achieve in the 2003 match against Namibia at Potchefstroom?
21) Which is the only ground being used in 2019 whose only ODIs have been World Cup matches?
22) Who has appeared in most finals but never batted?
23) Which country has been involved in the highest and lowest match (with a result) aggregates?
24) What stark difference was there between Chaminda Vaas's 2003 hat-trick and Steven Finn's in 2015?
25) Which player has taken most wickets without once taking five in an innings?
26) Which player with the record number of ODI ducks, never made one in the World Cup (and additionally was never dismissed in the 90s)?
27) Which player, on his birthday, scored his age?
28) The 1999 World Cup was held in venues in England, Wales, Scotland and Ireland and which other?
29) Which country did former Warwickshire and Glamorgan batsman, David Hemp, represent in the World Cup?
30) Which record does United Arab Emirates player, Amjad Javed, hold?

WORLD CUP QUIZ
ANSWERS

1) Headingley - Winston Davis (7-51 for West Indies vs. Australia in 1983) and Gary Gilmour (6-14 for Australia vs. England in 1975).
2) Four.
3) Arjuna Ranatunga for Sri Lanka vs. Australia in 1996.
4) Collins Obuya (5-24 Kenya vs Sri Lanka); Austin Codrington (5-27 Canada vs Bangladesh) and Rudi van Vuuren (5-43 Namibia vs England).
5) Kyle Coetzer 156 for Scotland vs Bangladesh at Nelson in 2015.
6) Cape Town against England in 2003. Nick Knight was the receiving batsman.
7) New Zealand (who have reached seven semi-finals but only one final).
8) Kenya in 2003.
9) India's Navjot Sidhu who made 73 against Australia at Madras.
10) Clive Lloyd (102 West Indies vs. Australia in 1975) and Ricky Ponting (140* Australia vs. India in 2003).
11) Taunton in 1999.
12) Scotland who have played in 14 matches.
13) 93 by West Indies against Kenya at Pune in 1996.
14) Ian Botham against South Africa at Sydney in 1992.
15) Graham Gooch (in 1979, 1987 and 1992).
16) Kenya's Thomas Odoyo with 23 in 25 matches.
17) Clive Lloyd in 1975; Ricky Ponting in 2003 and Mahendra Singh Dhoni in 2011.
18) Geoffrey Boycott who took five wickets at an average of 18.80.

19) He was the top-scorer and had the best bowling analysis in the match.
20) They all individually made more runs than the combined Namibian total of 45.
21) Taunton.
22) Australia's Glenn McGrath with four.
23) Sri Lanka. The highest is 688 for 18 wickets against Australia at Sydney in 2015 and the lowest 73 for 11 wickets against Canada at Paarl in 2003.
24) Vaas's came from the first three balls of the match whilst Finn's came from the last three balls of the innings.
25) Sri Lanka's Muttiah Muralitharan with 68 wickets.
26) Sri Lanka's Sanath Jayasuriya.
27) Andrew Strauss scored 34 on his 34th birthday against Ireland in Bangalore in 2011.
28) Amstelveen in Netherlands.
29) Bermuda.
30) He has twice featured in the joint-highest, seventh-wicket record World Cup partnership.

BIBLIOGRAPHY

Books including Yearbooks

BAXTER, Peter, *World Cup Cricket's Clash of the Titans* (Andre Deutsch Ltd 1999).

BROWNING, Mark and GRAPSAS, James, *A Complete History of World Cup Cricket* (New Holland Publishers 2004).

BRYDEN, Colin, *Return of the prodigal* (Sunday Times & Jonathan Ball Publishers 1992).

CRACE, John, *Wasim and Waqar: Imran's Inheritors* (Boxtree Limited 1993).

DE SILVA, Aravinda, *Aravinda, My Biography* (Mainstream Publishing Company (Edinburgh) Ltd. 1999)

FOWLER, Graham, *Absolutely Foxed* (Simon & Schuster UK Ltd 2017).

FRITH, David, *Thommo* (Angus & Robertson Publishers 1980).

GILCHRIST, Adam, *True Colours* (Pan Macmillan Australia Pty Ltd 2008).

HAWKINS, Ed, *Bookie, Gambler, Fixer, Spy* (Bloomsbury Publishing Plc 2012).

Indian Cricket 1983 (Kasturi & Sons, Madras).

Indian Cricket 1996 (Kasturi & Sons, Chennai).

JOHNSON, Martin and BLOFELD, Henry, *The* Independent *World Cup Cricket '* (The Kingswood Press).

MANDHANI, Pradeep, *Cricket World Cup '99 Frozen* (Parshva Offset Press, New Delhi 2000).

WARNE, Shane and NICHOLAS, Mark, *No Spin* (Ebury Press 2018).

OLONGA, Henry, *Blood, Sweat and Treason* (Vision Sports Publishing 2011).

PONTING, Ricky, *At the Close of Play* Ricky Ponting (HarperCollins Publishers 2013).

PROCTER, Mike, *South Africa: The Years of Isolation and the Return to International Cricket* (Queen Anne Press 1994).

Prudential Cup Review: The Official Record of the 1979 Prudential Cup (A Sportsline production from Ramcroft Ltd.)

Sealed With a Six: The Story of the 2011 World Cup ESPN CRICINFO (Hachette India).

Sportsweek's *Book of the Reliance Cup* (Mid-Day Publications Pvt. Ltd, Bombay).

TAYLOR, James, *Cut Short* (Pen & Sword 2018).

WINDER, Robert, *Hell for Leather* (Victor Gollancz An imprint of the Cassell Group 1996).

WISDEN CRICKETERS' ALMANACK 1972, 1976, 1980, 1984, 1988, 1993, 1997, 2000, 2004, 2008, 2012 and 2016 (John Wisden & Co. Ltd).

Internet

TASTATS (www.tastats.com.au)

INDEX